THE LOST SCOTCH II

Further tales of MONEY & Strife

More stories, more twists, more halacha

THE LOST SCOTCH II

RABBI AVROHOM BOOKMAN

Further tales of MONEY & Strife

More stories, more twists, more halacha

Distributed by
ISRAEL BOOK SHOP
501 Prospect Street
Lakewood NJ 08701
Tel. 732-901-3009
Fax. 732-901-4012

www.Israelbookshoppublications.com

J.A. Bookman
225 14th Street
Lakewood NJ 08701

thelostscotch@hotmail.com

ISBN 978-1-60091-093-7

PRINTED IN CANADA

לע"נ

ר' מאיר נתן בן מנחם אריה ע"ה

מרת רחל בת נחום יצחק ע"ה

לע"נ

ר' יצחק צבי בן נחום הלוי ע"ה

מרת בשא בת עזרא ע"ה

קרן אברהם שמואל להדפסת ספרים
של ת"ח בעיר לייקוואוד
לע"נ אברהם שמואל בן הערשל

לכבוד דודינו המחבר ומשפחתו שיחיו
מאת
הדסה ,אלי ,אריה, פנינה,
מתי, שעי'

Contents

בס"ד

בית · מדרש · גבוה
Beth Medrash Govoha
בית מדרשו של רבנו הגאון רבי אהרן קוטלר זצוק"ל
Rabbi Aaron Kotler Institute for Advanced Learning
617 Sixth Street, Lakewood, NJ 08701 • (732) 367-1060 • Fax: (732) 367-7487

יום א' לפר' שמות תשס"ט

שמחתי מאד לראות שידידי הנעלה והיקר הרה"ג ר' אברהם בוקמן שליט"א הולך מחיל אל חיל ועומד עכשיו להוציא לאור עוד חיבור יפה מאד על עניני חושן משפט.

הרה"ג ר' אברהם שליט"א הוא ממצויני האברכים בבית מדרש גבוה בליקוואוד שמשים לילות כימים בעמל התורה הק' ועוסק בה ביגיעה עצומה הרבה שנים, ובשנים אחרונים הוא עוסק בהל' חושן משפט ביחד עם הרבה אברכים חשובים וידיו רב לו בפלפולא דאורייתא ובמו"מ של הלכה לאסוקי שמעתתא אליבא דהלכתא ולערוך מערכות לברר וללבן בבהירות ובמתיקות ענינים חמורים בחו"מ. ובעז"ה כבר הצליח לחבר חיבור חשוב. ובכשרונותיו הגדולים הוא מבהיר בספרו ענינים חמורים בחושן משפט על פי משלים וסיפורים שתכליתם לעורר בני אדם עד כמה נוגע דיני חו"מ על כל צד ושעל. והספר הביא תועלת גדולה שעל ידו התעוררו הרבה בני אדם לדקדק יותר על עניני חושן משפט. ושמעתי שהח"ח זצ"ל עורר בני הישיבה שבתפילת נעילה אנו מתפללים "למען נחדל מעושק ידינו". ואמרו חז"ל (בויק"ר לג' ג') ר"ש בר אבא בשם ר' יוחנן משל לסאה שהיא מלאה עונות מי מקטרג בה גזל. לכן באנו בזה לחזק ידי ידידי הנעלה שיצליח מאד להוסיף כהנה בחיבוריו היפים לזכות הרבים. ויזכה לישב באהלה של תורה כל ימיו, ללמוד וללמד ולהרביץ תורה והוראה בישראל מתוך מנוחת הנפש והרחבת הדעת ושמחה ונחת.

הכו"ח לכבוד התורה ולומדיה

ירוחם אלשין

ירוחם אלשין

ישראל מאיר גרינברג
רב דק"ק וביהמ"ד גולדרס גרין
לונדון יצ"ו

Yisroel Meir Greenberg
Golders Green Beth Hamedrash

בס"ד

יום ה' לפ' וארא שנת תשס"ט לפ"ק

הנה כבוד גיסי המכובד הרב הגאון המופלג טובא איש אשכולות בתורה ויראה הר"ר אברהם בוקמן שליט"א קפץ והחזיק בקרן התורה המונח בקרן זוית להעמידה ולהחזירה ליושנה חלק השו"ע חו"מ הנוגע למעשה בכל יום ויום וכבר בזמן החז"ל אמרו רובן בגזל ומה נאמר בעולם ההפקר שהגיענו בעוה"ר בזמנינו

וכן ע' בטור ריש חו"מ בגודל מעלת הדין והמשפט בין אדם לחבירו שהוא יסוד ועיקר בדול בעבודת ה' וכמו שאמרו חז"ל בב"ב קעה: שאין לך מקצוע בתורה יותר מהן וכבר כתב המהר"ל בדרך חיים כי עיקר המשפטים שהם בתורה הם הדינים

ובכל זה אחר יגיעה רבה ועמלה לברר וללבן דיני תורה על בורים שמעתתא אליבא דהלכתא זכה מר כ"ת לחבר עוד חיבור נאה ויפה בלשון צח ומקובל ומובן לכל חלקי כלל ישראל הכל דין תורה לאמיתו לעורר ולמשוך לב כל הקוראים בו לדקדק בדיני ממונות כדבעי וזכות חיבור כזה גדול מאד

ויה"ר שיהיו לו ס"ד להמשיך לעיין ולחבר עוד ספרים קדושים ולהפיץ תורה לרבים וזכות כל הנ"ל יגן לו שיראה בתוך ביתו רק נחת וברכה מכל צאצאיו אכי"ר

החותם בהוקרה ובברכה

RABBINICAL COURT
MAYSHARIM
GUIDED BY RABBI NISSIM KARELITZ
BAIS DIN TZEDEK OF BNEI BRAK

בית דין צדק
מישרים
בהכוונת בית דין צדק - בני ברק
בראשות מרן הגאון **רבי נסים קרליץ** שליט"א

בס"ד

כ"ט יום לחדש טבת תשס"ט לפ"ק

הנני להגיד לאדם יושרו, ה"ה ידידי ורב חביבי, הרה"ג הנעלה, מרביץ תורה לעדרים, מוהר"ר יהונתן אברהם בוקמן שליט"א, אשר הרבה מקנתו במקצוע הלכות ממונות שבשו"ע חו"מ, בשבת תחכמוני דבי אולפנא רבתא דבית מדרש גבוה בעיה"ת ליקוואוד יצ"ו, ובמשך השנים עסקנו יחד הרבה במו"מ של הלכה וראיתי רב חילו ברוחב ידיעותיו ובאסוקי שמעתתא אליבא דהלכתא, בטוב טעם ודעת, כיד ה' הטובה עליו.

ומיגו דזכי לנפשיה זכי נמי לחבריה, בחיבור ספר בלשון אנגלית המדוברת, בו שיכל את ידיו להציע יסודות הלכתיים ע"י סיפורים ערוכים במיטב הגיון, סובבים על צירי שאלות הלכתיות ומצבים שונים הנוגעים לענייני חו"מ, וכל זאת במטרה ללמד דעת את העם, באופן שגם הציבור הרחב ואף נשים וצעירי ישראל יוכלו להפיק לקח ולהתעורר למכשולות נפוצים בעניינים אלו, ולהתרגל לדקדק בדרכיהם ולבררם ע"פ דבר ה' זו הלכה בכל עסקי משאם ומתנם עם הזולת ובכל אורחות החיים בעולם המעשה.

זכה ידידי הנ"ל ליטול חלקו השמור לו בחיזוק עמודי ההלכה ע"י ספרו הראשון שנתקבל בקרב שכבות הציבור. וכעת, לאור הצלחתו הראשונה בזה, הריהו נותן לפנינו ברכה בחיבור שני באותה דרך. ולא נצרך אלא לברכת ידיד, שכמעשהו בראשונה כן אף בשנית ייאצל עליו חסד ה', בסייעתא דשמיא לביצוע הגיון לבו הטוב, להעמיד ולקיים שמירת הלכות ממונות כדת וכדין, וזכות הרבים שמורה לו לעד לשפע ברכה והצלחה, ברוב טוב ובנעימים,

כעתירת ידידו דורש שלומו וטובתו תמיד,

יששכר דוב הכהן כהנא

יששכר דוב הכהן כהנא

אב"ד בי"ד מישרים, ליקוואוד יצ"ו

Office & Mailing Address: 625 Forest Avenue, Lakewood, N.J. 08701 • **Telephone:** 732.905.3388 • **Fax:** 732.905.5880

לשכות הבד"צ: **Rabbinical Courtrooms:** 625 Forest Avenue, Lakewood, N.J. (Rear Entrance)
2913 Avenue L, Brooklyn, N.Y. (Lower Level)

בס"ד

דוד גרוסמן
כולל זכרון גרשון
בית הוועד לעניני משפט
לייקוואוד, נ. דז.

RABBI DOVID GROSSMAN
Kollel Zichron Gershon
Bais HaVaad L'Inyonei Mishpat
32 Fifth Street
Lakewood, N.J. 08701

הנני בזה לשבח המגיע לכתבים, אודות האי גברא רבה, יושב ומעמיק באוהלה של תורה, יושב בבית מדרשינו ידידי הרב ר' אברהם בוקמן שליט"א אשר מסר לבו ונפשו להעמיק בעומק של תורה, וזכה לשנן לחדד ולבהיר עד שיצא מתחת ידו את "דבר ה' -זו הלכה" וכדי להרביץ וללמד להמונם נתן מנפשו להגיש מהסולת הנקי' ספר זה שמושך לב הקוראים ומעורר לבם של אלו שרוב עסקיהם נוגעים להל' חושן משפט ונתן להם כלי מוכשר לעזור להם ללמוד וללמד לשמור ולעשות את דברי תלמוד תורת ה' באהבה.

יה"ר שהשי"ת יעזור לו שיוכל להמשיך בעבודתו יתברך להעמיק בעמילות ויגיע לעסוקי שמעתתא אליבא דהלכתא מתוך בריות גופא ונהורא מעליא מתוך הרחבת הדעת, עד ביאת גואל בב"א.

דוד גרוסמן

דוד גרוסמן

בס"ד

מכתב ברכה

הנני בזה לחזק את ידי הרב החשוב ר' אברהם בוקמן שליט"א שמפליא בפעולתיו מעשה ידי אומן לכתוב בשפה המדוברת סיפורים שיש בהם ממש ללמוד הלכה למעשה בדינים בן אדם לחבירו.

הרי זה נדבך נוסף במשימה הנעלה להעיר לב הציבור בדברים העומדים ברומו של עולם כאשר מתוך העיון והמשא ומתן בדבריו יתבררו ויתלבנו ההוראות האיך להתנהג בעובדות כאלה.

ובזה הנני לברך את הרב המחבר שליט"א שיוסיף לזכנו בחיבורים מחוכמים כאשר עשה עד עתה, ויהיה בזה ממזכה הרבים שזכות הרבים הקוראים ולומדים את דבריו תלוי בו.

חיים קאהן

Preface

The Court's work was almost complete. All that remained was the reading of the verdict after which sentencing would take place. As the Judge's voice rang out strong and true, Solly Weinreb held his head low. There was no more hiding, no more deception- he had finally been unmasked and would now have to suffer the consequences of his actions.

"If any person has information to share with this court they should step forth now." The proclamation sounded out more as a matter of rote than genuine anticipation for seldom, if ever, did it elicit any response.

"There is actually one small anecdote I would like to retell," a quiet voice spoke out from the rear of the courtroom. All eyes turned to see the small bent-over frame of an old, frail woman clad in a worn shawl and wearing a torn kerchief as a head covering. While seemingly surprised at this intrusion the Judge maintained his bearing, continuing unflinchingly with courtroom protocol.

"Could you please present yourself to the court and explain your business in Mr. Weinreb's case?" He requested.

"Aidel Bloch, wife of one Rabbi Zische Bloch," she answered. "Many years ago my husband opened a bakery in

Mr. Weinreb's apartment complex," she explained. "The work was hard and the profits slim, but we were at least able to make ends meet. Then tragedy struck and my husband died, leaving me to care for our family.

Running the bakery whilst simultaneously caring for my children was excruciatingly difficult but we still managed to eke by, somehow surviving through even the coldest of winters. This continued for some years and I was always able to pay Mr. Weinreb our monthly rent on time.

Now although I was aware that Mr. Weinreb had not raised the rent since my husband died I had not given it much thought until one day Mr. Weinreb himself came into the store looking nervous and concerned. Hesitatingly, he explained that times had changed and he had no option but to raise our rent. There was a huge demand for stores in our area and he had other customers willing to pay even double what I was paying. He gave us three months to agree to the demand or find other premises, but I couldn't do either so instead we went to a Din Torah. I explained to the *Dayonim* our situation but it didn't help. Mr. Weinreb was giving us ample warning, he was still charging below the regular price and if we wanted to be recipients of charity it wasn't his responsibility more than anyone else's to support us. The *Dayonim* finally ruled that Mr. Weinreb was indeed correct and had every *Halachic* right to evict us.

We waited. All that needed to be done to enforce our eviction was Mr. Weinreb's word, but mysteriously that word never came. Month after month we continued paying the original rent and not another word about the matter was heard."

Mrs. Bloch ended her story here but still the puzzle remained incomplete. Why indeed had Solly, after winning his Din Torah, not followed through with the *psak Halacha* and evict his underpaying tenant? What had occurred that had changed his heart? These questions were put to the defendant who quietly explained what had transpired.

"Although I had won the Din Torah I felt uncomfortable about evicting the widow Bloch and her family," Solly began. "On the other hand the amount of rent I was losing exceeded my charitable obligations for the month and I could hardly afford to maintain the subsidy without threatening my entire business. Not knowing what to do I wrote to my Rebbe and his reply came in the form of a postcard upon which was written the following.

"Know well that you are perfectly entitled to follow the dictates of the Shulchan Aruch and follow through with the psak of the Dayonim. This is your right and something your litigants well understood when they came before the Beis Din *together with you. But be warned. There will come a time when you yourself will be held accountable for following the dictates of Halacha. On that Day of Judgment you will be held responsible for even the most minor of Halachic infringements. However, if today you grant the widow Bloch reprieve from her Halachic obligation, a similar standard will be accorded to you on your judgement day in the future."*

That is what the Rebbe wrote to me on the postcard," Solly finally concluded, "and that is why Mrs. Bloch was able to come and testify on my behalf today."[1]

☞ *The Heavenly Tribunal seemed well pleased with Solly's decision not to evict the widow Bloch. Does that mean the Beis Din were wrong to rule in his favor?* *(p.209)*

---

1. I heard this story from Rabbi Yedidya Einhorn שליט"א who heard it from Reb Yankele Leizer זצ"ל who heard it from his father-in-law Reb Itzekele Gewirtzman זצ"ל who saw the actual postcard as written by the Chechenever Rebbe זי"ע, son of the Shinover Rebbe זי"ע.

Acknowledgements

I am grateful to my wife and extended family for tolerating both the production of this volume and fallout from the first. Not being of Scottish extraction (for the most part), they bear less resilience to the many tribal and cocktail slurs that have arisen since its publication.

I am grateful to our Rosh Kollel in Beth Medrash Govoha, Rabbi Yehoshua Krupenia shlita and the other many talmidei chachomim who form the makeup of our Chabura. A list of their names can be found in the excellent work Business Halacha, authored by my colleague Rabbi Ari Marburger.

I would like to thank Rabbis Doniel Harris, David Manovic and Shlomo Zafrani for their readily available input, advice, encouragement and assistance, without which this book would still be far from completion.

As in the first book, my brother Adam took great pains to ensure the correctness and accuracy of this volume, efforts for which I am very much indebted.

Thanks are also owed to Rabbis Moshe Friedmann, Zev Roth, Avrohom Jaffe, Aharon Rottenberg, Yeshaya Meir Bassman, Melech Josephson, Dovid Gestetner, Naftoli Wayntraub, Rabbi Dov Kahan of Bais Din Maysharim, Rabbi Dovid Grossman of Kollel Zichron Gershon, and also to Rabbis Moshe Kaufman and Chaim Boruch Wolf of Israel Book Shop.

Finally I would like to take this opportunity to thank my esteemed brother-in-law Rabbi Moshe Litke and family for their untiring and perceptive efforts on my, and my family's behalf. Dedicating this book in their honor is but a small measure of gratitude for all we have gained.

1

The Wedding Drummer

Zvi Steinman had made sure his wedding would be one to remember. Not only was the inimitable Chaim ben Zundel singing at the microphone but the great Benny Bongo (not his real name) was also on stage, playing in the band. And what a show the two of them gave! Chaim's powerful voice and infectious enthusiasm soon had nearly everyone dancing and Benny Bongo's masterful control of the drumsticks ensured everyone's steps kept in perfect beat.

Ari Borden was one of the non-dancers. He had spent only a few minutes circling the *chosson* on the parquet floor before breaking away and moving towards the stage where the band was performing. Positioning himself squarely in front of the drummer, he watched with deep concentration as Benny's arms flashed wildly in seemingly random patterns. Yet the remarkably rhythmic sounds produced by the tall and lanky drummer gave lie to such notion, as it was clear that every beat was well predicated with careful calculation.

Another guest observing Benny's energetic movements was a middle-aged Menachem Lanning. Standing at a safer distance next to the *mechitza* he watched in awe as Benny, with unstoppable energy conducted a grand, hand-flying, cymbal-bashing, drum-beating, session ending finale. Sighing audibly after its breathtaking conclusion, Menachem suddenly became aware of another, more urgent tapping upon his shoulder from the other side of the *mechitza*.

"WHOAAAAHH! Oh Ma, it's you!" he exclaimed, recovering from the original shock of the sensation.

"Yes it's me, and why weren't you dancing along with everyone else?" demanded an elder Mrs. Lanning.

"Ma, I was before," explained Menachem meekly, "but I just needed a little break and anyhow all these new dances...."

"Never mind that," interrupted his mother. "I don't really care too much. What I would like to know is who is that over there?" she asked, pointing in the direction of the band.

"Why, that's Benny Bongo, Ma," replied Menachem, pleasantly surprised at his mother's youthful musical appreciation. "Good, isn't he!"

"I don't mean that infernally noisy drummer Menachem," she retorted sharply. "What could you have been thinking dear! I mean the short young man over there standing next to the stage. He looks like a nice boy, maybe just what your cousin Bashy is looking for. Perhaps you could find out who he is?"

Sensing a need to prove his mettle, Menachem immediately executed this reconnaissance by strolling over to Ari and plucking up a casual conversation.

"Great band here tonight, no?" remarked Menachem. "And especially that drummer. This is the first time I've seen him in action and he's really good."

"Good?!" exclaimed Ari. "Benny Bongo's one of the best there is. And did you ever see such a drum set?" he added, surveying Benny's equipment. "It must be worth in the thousands. That's a custom paint finish and all the skins are top quality. You can hear it in the sound if you listen carefully."

"Really!" replied Menachem vaguely, his eyes glazing over in a haze of confusion. "I was just impressed at how fast his hands were moving."

"That's his hands *and* his feet," corrected Ari. "Benny plays with a double bass drum and it takes a lot of skill to switch from the hi-hat to the double-bass without skipping a beat."

"Double-bass?" questioned Menachem, now totally out of his depth.

"Yeah! It's spelled B-A-S-S. It means he hits that big drum with two pedals at the same time. Anyhow, I have to go now. I see the waiters are by my table already and I don't want to miss dinner. 'Bye and nice meeting you."

"Sorry, I didn't catch your name?" Menachem managed to ask before Ari departed.

"Ari Borden. I'm a cousin of the *chosson*," he added, quickly turning after the yearnings of his stomach before Menachem could delay him further.

Mrs. Lanning had been watching the entire encounter from across the hall and waited impatiently as Menachem made his way through the tables and back towards her at the *mechitza*.

"Well, what happened then?" she asked as he came within earshot.

"His name's Ari Borden," reported Menachem, "and he's a cousin of the *chosson*."

"Borden...Ari Borden....." repeated Mrs. Lanning slowly, her gaze focusing upon an imaginary object in the distance. "He must be Jules and Stephanie's boy then," she finally said. "Excellent Menachem, good work. Just leave it with me and I'll see what we can do about this."

True to her word Mrs. Lanning went about putting her grand idea into motion that very next day. The quintessential *bubby-tante-shadchan*, her poise was perfect for laying the groundwork for a successful shidduch and she soon had the consent of both sets of parents. All that now lay between the young couple she felt were a few successful meetings and then the match could be announced.

Alas, this last piece of the puzzle proved to be more elusive. An initial meeting between Ari and Bashy proved rather dismal and uninspiring, leaving Mrs. Lanning with the difficult task of trying to keep the *shidduch* afloat.

"But Ari seems like such a nice boy to me," repeated Mrs. Lanning to Bashy during a supportive conversation. "I'm sure that if you'll just relax and trust your great-aunt's sixth sense you'll see his qualities. At least give it one more meeting, won't you dear?"

Reluctantly, Bashy acquiesced for what she envisioned to be a final farewell meeting with Ari, solely for the sake of her octogenarian aunt. Naturally, such a negative attitude to their upcoming meeting lay the groundwork for an almost inevitable disappointing dating experience.

They met the following Thursday evening and again Bashy found their conversation to be stilted and unnatural with Ari seeming to hold opposing views on most of the topics they discussed. In fact, the only redeeming part of the evening was when Ari, obviously sharing her sentiments, suggested winding down the date earlier than could have normally been expected.

"I should have known better than to trust Tante Esther's intuition," Bashy silently berated herself as they entered the car for the drive home. "If I could only have just said 'no' to this guy at the beginning I wouldn't have ended up wasting these two nights."

However, Bashy's relief that the experience was finally ending proved to be a tad premature. Rather than a quick and speedy ride home, Ari and Bashy soon found themselves caught up in the midst of a most horrendous traffic jam. Painstakingly, their vehicle inched forward ever so slowly as the two sat together, cloaked in a tense, deafening silence.

Then, as the car in front of theirs ground to a halt once again, Ari began his subconscious habit of rhythmically tapping his fingers upon the steering wheel as if it were a set of drum pads. His prowess at this task was instantly apparent and Bashy was quite taken with the smooth and even tones resonating forth.

"Hey, that's a really good beat you've got going there!" she said quite naturally; actually it was probably the most natural thing she had said all night. "Where did you learn to drum like that?"

Horrified at himself Ari instantly threw his fingers around the steering wheel grasping it as tightly as his hands could bear. Swallowing deeply he managed to eke out a humble response.

"It….it was nothing really," he explained in extreme embarrassment. "Just a simple little beat I was trying out."

"You must play the drums then, right?" she asked inquisitively. "That wasn't just any amateur tapping you were doing."

"Yes, you're right," conceded Ari. "I do actually, but really only very occasionally. Like at the yeshiva's Purim event or Chanukah party. When I was a kid I used to play much more but I don't really have the time now."

"That's really funny," added Bashy interestedly. "When I was younger my parents wanted me to take up music, but it really wasn't my style so we made a compromise and *I* also learned to play the drums. Now I'm forever kept busy playing at girls' choirs and shows."

"Have you seen this new drummer Benny Bongo on the wedding scene recently?" Ari then asked. "He's really something special."

"Yeah, he's a real professional," confirmed Bashy. "We saw him playing at my friend's *chassuna* last week."

"They say he used to play for an Italian rock band before he became *frum*."

"Italian?" questioned Bashy. "I heard it was a French one, from Paris actually."

Sensibly, Ari took a non-aggressive stance to this challenge upon the accuracy of his information.

"Italy? France? Rumors like these always go around and no-one ever really finds out the truth. For all we know he might just as well come from Bognor Regis," he chuckled.

"From where?" asked Bashy.

"Bognor Regis. It's just a plain, non-descript seaside resort near Bournemouth in England. I was there last year with my family."

"That's cool! We were also there although that was two years ago. Cute little place, no?"

"Yeah, kind of, once you get used to the accent! Oh hullo there I say," Ari began in a grossly exaggerated impersonation of the Englishman's vernacular. "Have a good day sir! Jolly good! Champion, no what?"

While this derisive mimicry would only have succeeded in enraging any British native, Bashy actually find it quite amusing.

"Yes I know what you mean," she agreed wholeheartedly. "But it's still quite a quaint little place nonetheless, don't you think?"

This only gave Ari something else to agree with,

"Sure, we actually had a great time there," and so continued the conversation between the two long after the traffic holdup had cleared.

By the time they had arrived back at Bashy's home both her and Ari had realized the need to second-think abandoning the *shidduch,* a sentiment Bashy shyly acknowledged to her parents that night.

"I'm not saying we're getting engaged or anything like that," she hastily added. "but I just need to make sure it's really a 'no'."

Even with this professed lack of interest, it still took no more than a fortnight for Bashy's failing experience to turn around and develop from amiable courtship to joyous engagement.

"I told you it was a good idea," Esther Lanning eagerly told all at the *l'chaim*. "There are some things about which an elderly aunt just seems to know best!" and while Ari and Bashy wholeheartedly agreed with her about each other, they did share her thoughts regarding their wedding band. That was something quite different, a matter which Ari was to attend to with the help of a useful phone number passed on by one of his friends.

"Hello, Family Bengio, how can I help you?"

"Oh! Excuse me. Is…is that seven four two, zero three eight five. I think I may have dialed the wrong number."

"No that's correct. Who are you looking for?"

"I was actually looking for the famous drummer Benny Bongo."

"One second please, while I call my husband………… BEINUSH! YOU HAVE A PHONE CALL."

Ari waited a few seconds before a male voice appeared on the end of the receiver, with a distinctly European accent.

"Yes zis is Benny Bongo. 'ow can I help you?"

"Yes, my name's Ari Borden and I'm getting married in two months, on the twenty fourth of June. Would you be available then to come and play for us on that date?"

"Let me just check ze date for you. Yes it seems to be free," confirmed Benny. "Do you know which band you are using so we can clear it with zem also?"

"Yes. It's the Kinor Band."

"Okay, zat should be fine. I play with zem a lot. Now my fee for a wedding iz one zousand dollars and you should make sure to pay me directly."

"Yes, I know. My father's only taking care of Kinor, so I'd have to pay you separately anyhow."

"Good, excellent. Zo, I zink we're all set zen for ze twenty force."

"Wonderful! Thank you very much. My kallah will be so happy to hear that you're coming."

"Just make you tell Kinor you've spoken to me so zey don't bring a drummer of zeir own."

"Okay, we will do for sure."

☙ ☙ ☙

The twenty fourth of June proved to be a most propitious day for a wedding. The weather was warm, dry and not too humid. The guests were in a relaxed pre-vacation disposition and Ari's friends were in the best of spirits, fully enjoying all the hype of the summer wedding season.

After a moving *chuppah* ceremony (and some rushed family photographs,) an ecstatic Ari and Bashy burst out onto the dance floor launching the *simcha* into high gear. Their excitement was contagious and soon all were enthusiastic participants in the fast-paced dancing, expertly orchestrated through the talent-filled hands of Benny Bongo and the other members of the Kinor Band.

A riveting, trademark finale indicated the end of the first dance after which the guests were given a short break during which to refresh and enjoy the sumptuous dinner being served. A few, slower-paced, musical scores served as welcome accompaniment and then, after twenty minutes they were ready to recommence the dancing. Once again, with the *bochurim* leading the way, all were caught up in the spirited and energy-filled atmosphere of the *simcha*.

It was midway through this second dance that the prodding began.

"Come on Ari, let's hear you on the drums," suggested Chaim Jacoby as the circle of dancers closed in around the *chosson*.

"Yeah!" agreed Sruly Teitlebaum. "Let's hear it for the kallah!"

As these sentiments echoed louder amongst his friends, Ari's own interest in the idea grew and he soon found himself being propelled towards the stage where the band was playing. Soon, the group of clapping *bochurim* accompanying Ari was standing directly in front of Benny Bongo who looked up in understanding acknowledgement of their inferred request. With an experienced smile, he stood up from the narrow stool, moved to the side and, in a most opulent gesture, handed Ari the two drumsticks.

Taking the initiative Ari seated himself at the drums and with a fair measure of proficiency began to strike up a pleasantly intelligible level of percussion. He struck out confidently, first at the snare drum, then at the cymbals, then back again to the snare drum, with ever increasing strength and velocity, much to the delight of his cheering friends.

News of his antics soon reached the *kallah's* ears and, wanting to see the sight for herself, she found a gap in the *mechitza* to spy out her new husband in action. Seeing his *kallah* appear only energized Ari further and with increasing vigor and intensity, his drumming took on an even more desperate and accelerated beat.

Now, as has been mentioned earlier in this narrative, Benny Bongo was of the rather tall creed whilst simultaneously Ari, our *chosson* was of rather shorter stock. While this disparity is largely irrelevant in most day-to-day situations it does have rather important ramifications in the realm of drumming stools and in particular to their height adjustments. Hence, while it was that Benny Bongo could reach his drum pedals with ease Ari, perched atop this selfsame stool with his considerably shorter legs was much more taxed in trying to achieve this same aim.

It was in such circumstance that our adrenalin-infused *chosson* made a reckless stab for that elusive specialty of Benny Bongo, the rhythmic-crunching double bass. He stretched out his foot, made contact with the pedal and sounded the drum but the force of the rebound spring proved too much for his fragile position at the edge of the narrow stool. Caught off balance Ari threw back his arms wildly in a vain attempt to remain upright but the effort failed and he ended up lying flat on his back, the stool overturned beside him.

The crowd gasped. Even the band was stunned into frozen silence and all that could be heard was the cacophonic sound of various drumming components crashing down upon each other and the floor in haphazard percussion. All eyes peered towards the hapless *chosson* who, although momentarily shocked quickly regained his composure. With smiling eyes and a boyish grin Ari soon reassured all that he was quite unharmed in the event beckoning his friends to return with him to the dance floor.

As he stood up, the bandleader motioned his men to pick up a calming song and Ari, together with his entourage, gradually made their way off the stage. Even the *kallah* quickly recovered her smile after the initial shock but there remained one individual quite overcome at what had transpired.

"OH LALALA!" cried out Benny, reverting unconsciously back to his mother tongue. "QUELLE CATASTROPHE! QUELLE CATASTROPHE!" he muttered over and over as he turned to the task of reassembling his drum set-up.

But the damage done to its components during the accident were so crippling as to prevent this from being properly executed. The hi-hat cymbal had been bent badly out of shape and the percussion bracket had also sustained serious damage. Worst of all though was the ugly scratch afflicted onto the side of the big bass drum. Repairing it would be costly indeed, as Benny Bongo made sure to point out to Ari's father.

"Zis damaje is very expensive to fix," he angrily pointed out. "and someone is now going to have to pay me fifteen 'undred dollars more to cover ze costs of ze repair."

"FIFTEEN HUNDRED DOLLARS!" exclaimed Ari's father. "YOU MUST BE JOKING! I can't pay you that kind of money. You're charging my son enough for playing here altogether and to start tagging on other fees because of a small mishap is completely uncalled for. On the contrary, we should all just be happy that the *chosson* wasn't harmed in the incident rather than using it as a money extortion ploy."

"But ze damaje...... ze damaje........," repeated Benny.

Alas, Mr. Borden was now no longer listening, having retreated out of earshot on to the distant dance floor.

☞ *Do Ari or his father have to pay for the damage done to Benny's drum set? (p. 211)*

2

Es-rogue

Meir Cooperstein was barely thirteen years old when he first truly discovered *Esrogim*. It had started one Ellul when a favorite teacher, Rabbi Haddar decided to educate his class in the fine art of identifying and selecting an appropriate specimen for the upcoming *Yom Tov* of Succos.

"Not all *esrogim* are equal," Rabbi Haddar had begun. "In fact, not all *esrogim* are *esrogim* altogether!" he added trying to pique the class's interest. "Common practice amongst the populace is to select a fruit solely based on looks. If the color is good, the shape uniform and the skin free from blemishes most people will be content to pay well and use their *esrog* proudly on *Yom Tov*. However, this approach neglects to consider one very important aspect: *yichus*."

While many of the boys in the class remained decidedly uninterested in the veritable bombshell that had just been dropped, Meir was fascinated. He knew that his family could trace their lineage back to the medieval scholar Rashi but having *esrogim* also trace back their roots sounded like a subject too fascinating to daydream through. He listened avidly as the teacher continued.

"There are many different authentic orchards spread out across the globe but there are also many *esrog* impersonators too. These are trees which *look* like *esrog* trees but grafting and other human interference could have tampered with the original *esrog* DNA producing a different fruit with certain characteristics merely *similar* to those of an *esrog*. Hence, the conscientious and punctilious individual will be sure to only select an *esrog* from a tried and true orchard whose authenticity has been validated by Jews from previous generations."

"But which one is the best?" asked Meir raising his hand. "Why can't everyone just use the best one and forget about all the others?"

"Meir, that is an excellent question," responded Rabbi Haddar warmly. "I'm glad that at least someone has been listening. The answer is that different people have different opinions as to which orchard *is* the most authentic one. Some people will only use an *esrog* from a particular orchard in Tiberius. Others are convinced that Tunisian *esrogim* are the most genuine. Still others wax enthusiastic for Californian specimens and so on. Each have their own special qualities making it impossible to say definitively that one is necessarily any better than another."

"So which one should I use then?" asked Ari further. "I can't afford to buy one from *every* orchard just to make sure!"

Rabbi Haddar chuckled upon hearing Ari's conundrum and explained that the problem was not new.

"What some people do is 'borrow' other people's *esrogim* on the first day of *Yom Tov*. You just find someone who has an *esrog* with a different *yichus* than the one you've bought and then use it to shake for a minute. That way you can fulfill the *Mitzvah* according to as many different opinions as there are different *esrogim* in your *shul*."

ଔ ଔ ଔ

Meir took his *esrog* lesson very much to heart and, despite his tenderness in years, spent a good deal of time that Succos borrowing his *shul* members' various *esrogim*. Some were amused by his actions and others more mystified but Meir's youthful innocence and sincerity endeared him to all, enabling his quest to be carried out with favorable results.

In subsequent years the *shul* members already knew what to expect from Meir and were even quietly proud when he would approach and ask to use their *esrog*.

Similarly enchanted by the budding young expert were the *esrog* merchants in town who equally treasured the prize of receiving Meir's custom. Although of limited resources, Meir would patiently go from store to store with all the carriage of a connoisseur many years his senior. Each one's wares would be lovingly scrutinized and examined before Meir would finally decide upon a fruit that matched both his wants and his budget.

The years passed and within time Meir himself became a proverbial *esrog*. A fine looking young man from good stock, matchmakers eagerly sought his attention with any number of equally eligible and well thought-of young women. Putting monetary concerns aside his deliberations led him to Grantsburg, Wisconsin where he met Peri, a quiet, sweet-natured girl from a very fine, simple family. The *shidduch* was soon completed and within time the young couple were happily married and living together in Meir's hometown on the East Coast.

With the passing of their first summer together came the dilemma of where to spend Succos. Both sets of parents offered gracious invitations and Meir and Peri toyed with the idea of spending the first days with her parents in Grantsburg returning home during *chol hamoed* to spend the remainder of *Yom Tov* with Meir's family. Finalizing such an arrangement was the topic of discussion between them one morning over breakfast.

"I'll tell you what Peri," Meir commented to his wife thoughtfully. "How would you like to spend Yom Kippur in Grantsburg as well as the first days of Succos? I would feel funny flying in and then flying out again less than a week later. Maybe it would more appropriate to spend a little more time with your parents instead and I don't have much going on here that week anyway?"

Ever the loyal wife, Peri was happy to defer the decision to her noble husband.

"Meir, whatever you think best is fine," she replied, "But before we consider it further we'll need to make sure we can get seats there in *shul* for Yom Kippur. Last year the place was jam-packed and there were no empty places at all."

"So that decides it then," said Meir conclusively. "If we can get seats for *davening* then we'll go to your parents for Yom Kippur."

When Peri called her father later that day she found him unusually interested in their idea of an extended visit even before any mention of securing seats in the *shul*.

"Was this Meir's idea?" commented Chatzkel Greenbaum. "He really is so thoughtful although it's quite a coincidence that you're calling about this just now. Would you mind if I had a quick word with him perhaps?" he asked, without revealing just what it was that interested him so much.

More curious than concerned Peri happily obliged her father and graciously handed Meir the phone.

"Meir how are you doing? Of course we'd love to have you for Yom Kippur," said Mr. Greenbaum warmly. "As it happens I was considering calling you anyway about a development we had here and that maybe you'd be willing to help."

Meir listened politely as his father-in-law continued with a not too demanding request.

"I'm sure you must have seen at your wedding that Peri's grandfather was having trouble with his mobility. Well I'm afraid to say that he's not been doing so well these past few weeks and we were concerned that it might be too ambitious for him to *daven* in our regular *shul* over the *Yomim Noraim*. Instead we planned on *davening* with him here at home and although we could probably muster together a *minyan* of strangers it would be a tremendous *chizzuk* for him if you and Peri would join us. I wasn't really going to ask, but since you were considering coming for Yom Kippur anyway it would be nice if you could make it a week earlier and come for Rosh Hashona also."

Mr. Greenbaum continued emphasizing how Meir shouldn't feel at all pressured to agree to the idea and that even being there for Yom Kippur alone would also be a tremendous help. But Meir and Peri were equal to the task, both agreeing that doing Peri's father's bidding would be but the smallest gesture in acknowledgement of the tremendous general efforts he extended on their behalf. There was only one small concern that Meir harbored.

"How about buying an *esrog* in Grantsburg though?" he asked. "I'm sure the store there sells them, but it means a lot to me to find a really special *esrog* and I normally rely on my contacts here."

"Relax Meir!" insisted Mr. Greenbaum. "Last year we had three or four people selling *esrogim* and this year there'll be even more. Don't worry you'll be able to find an *esrog* that meets your satisfaction, I guarantee it!"

ଔ ଔ ଔ

With map in hand and a car at his disposal Meir was ready to begin his annual quest. His father-in-law had kindly collated the names and addresses of all the *esrog* merchants in Grantsburg and with a long Tzom-Gedalyah afternoon ahead of him Meir got down to work.

At first he was disappointed. His first port of call had been Joseph's Judaica but the rather weak selection of *esrogim* on display was sadly uninspiring. Meir dutifully searched through the selections nonetheless but within an hour had dismissed them all for being both of poorer breed and inferior quality. The remainder of that first day was spent looking through the selections of Manny's Matanot and while the store certainly stocked *esrogim* of solid *yichus,* Meir remained unsatisfied.

The following day proved much more propitious. Jake's *Lulav* and *Esrog* Center presented a very large selection of quite handsome specimens and Meir had a thoroughly good time examining the different breeds and strains on offer. He looked at greener *esrogim,* more yellow fruits, ones with many bumps, hourglass-shaped *esrogim* with many from select, famous-name orchards. He even gave serious consideration to purchasing an *esrog* then and there, only holding himself back by considering there was still plenty of time and another three more names on his list.

It took Meir another two days to complete his reconnaissance until finally he felt confident enough with his knowledge of the market to at last make a purchase. Happy and excited, he returned back to his in-laws' home with the good news.

"Yes you were right," he confirmed to his father-in-law. "Grantsburg has some wonderful *esrogim* to choose from and I managed to get the *esrog* I wanted without even going too far over my budget." Proudly, he then held up a slightly yellow-tinged *esrog,* with many bumps, a strongly indented *ukatz* and an almost perfectly symmetrical, upright *pitom.* Mr. Greenbaum and indeed the entire Greenbaum family were happy with Meir's good fortune and shared in his eager enthusiasm for the first day of Succos when he would get to shake it.

ଔ ଔ ଔ

First day Succos:
Grantsburg Hebrew Congregation

Davening had finished, and while the *chazzan* had perhaps oversung his station, the congregation still remained in good spirits. As the members lined up to wish their Rabbi a good *Yom Tov*, Meir carried out his annual custom of tracking down all the different *esrogim* available in *shul*. His neighbor had a large Moroccan variety which Meir gratefully shook and a man two rows in front was equally proud of his fine Italian specimen. As Meir continued from row to row his father-in-law approached, gesturing towards him excitedly.

"Mr. Berman, our president has the most gorgeous *esrog* this year," he told Meir enthusiastically, "and I'm sure he'd be delighted to let you borrow it. Why not go and ask him?"

This news was more than enough to fire up Meir's enthusiasm and he speedily made his way to the front of the *shul* to join the line in front of where Mr. Berman sat. Even from a distance Meir was able to discern that his father-in-law had not been wrong and the Berman *esrog* was indeed very worthy of the honor it was being accorded. When eventually his turn came Meir picked up the *esrog*, held it firmly for a moment, shook it together with his *lulav* and then returned it safely to its quite elegant silver and mahogany *esrog* box.

"I must say, that's a top *esrog* you have there, Mr. Berman," Meir respectfully complimented his benefactor. "If I'm not mistaken it's a genuine Chazzon Yechezkel one, from the orchard in Rchov Hetzodor in Bnei Brak, right?"

Mr. Berman was quite taken aback at the precise, almost psychic accuracy of Meir's conjecture.

"Why, yes young man, I believe you are quite right. How.... How did you know that?"

Meir smiled sheepishly.

"I'm not so smart really," he politely explained. "It's just that I remember looking at this very same *esrog* last week when I was looking for one myself. You must have bought it from that store on the main street next to the pizzeria, right?"

"Quite right!" confirmed Mr. Berman. "That's Jake's *Esrog* Center."

"Yes, that was the name! If I remember correctly this *esrog* came in a sleeved cardboard box with polystyrene padding and a bright blue elastic band around the outside. And it's easily recognizable because at the *ukatz* there are two small indentations almost exactly opposite each other."

Mr. Berman turned over the *esrog* to check and, after a brief inspection, smiled broadly.

"Quite right again!" he replied. "I see your son-in-law really knows his stuff!" he added, turning to Mr. Greenbaum. "In the time it took me to select this *esrog* I hardly even noticed all those details myself."

"I would have bought it for myself," Meir continued, "but there was no way I could afford such an expensive *esrog*."

Mr. Berman smiled.

"I'm not surprised. Four hundred dollars is even more than I would normally spend. But for such an *esrog* how could I say no!"

Meir looked puzzled.

"Four hundred dollars?" he repeated, the words flowing almost involuntarily from his mouth. "Jake charged you *four* hundred dollars for that *esrog*?"

"Why....yes? Is there a problem?"

"Oh.....ohhhhh!" sighed Meir softly, his eyes darting desperately as the color slowly drained from his face. "No.......no problem," he finally stammered trying to steal away from the situation. But Mr. Berman wasn't ready to let his prized *esrog* be so calmly dismissed.

"You think maybe I overpaid?" he asked strongly. "For a beautiful *esrog* like this?" But no matter what Mr. Berman said, Meir remained non-committal over the issue of the price.

"I'm really not such an expert to be able to tell you what the correct price for an *esrog* should be," he quietly admitted.

"But nonetheless, you did see this same *esrog* for sale in Jake's store, right?"

"I....I think so."

"For four hundred dollars, right?"

Meir looked helplessly towards his father-in-law before responding, aware of the bombshell he was about to drop.

"No Mr. Berman, it was actually................. *three* hundred dollars."

Mr. Berman was ready to challenge this assertion, but something about Meir's calm, confident air made him reconsider.

"Are you *sure*?" he asked again.

"Ye......es!" confirmed Meir slowly. "Jake told me the price himself. Three hundred, I remember distinctly."

Now reality began to sink in and Mr. Berman was not a happy customer at all.

"I can't believe it!" he eventually sputtered. "That creep must have switched prices on me! Just wait 'til I get a hold of him after *Yom Tov*!" he growled menacingly.

☞ *Would Mr. Berman be entitled to a refund from Jake for the extra hundred dollars he was charged? (p. 214)*

☞ *Was Meir allowed to divulge to Mr. Berman that he was offered that same esrog for one hundred dollars less than Mr. Berman paid? (ibid)*

3

Uzi goes to Court

A Din Torah was inevitable. Although the issues between Uzi and the Benarroches were common and surmountable, flared tempers and a few strokes of bad fortune had soured their relationship to the point of leaving them incommunicado. Uzi had tried to put the affair behind him without success, as a close acquaintance tactfully brought to his attention.

"Uzi, what are you spacing out about this time?" asked Chanoch Bernfield. "You just missed that last *Kaddish*[1]?"

"Wh…wh….what? Spacing out?" asked Uzi. "Oh yeah, maybe."

"Was it about that building job again that went sour? The one with Benarroch?"

"I guess it was," conceded Uzi. "Do you know how much money he still owes me? Why can't he just pay rather than make such a fuss?"

1. closing supplication of prayer service

Ever the loyal friend, Chanoch determined to help ease his friend's tortured plight with a most obvious and simple suggestion.

"You know Uzi, you really should go to Beis Din and sort this thing out once and for all. Until you do it'll always be at the back of your mind, stopping you from focusing on more important things."

"But I can't afford to risk a Din Torah," Uzi objected. "Let's say I lose and then end up having to pay Benarroch money instead. I didn't really do anything wrong but who's to say I'll be able to prove that to the Beis Din."

"Well maybe you really do owe him the money," pointed out Chanoch. "I mean, isn't that what the Beis Din is meant to decide? If you really are wrong isn't it better to get it over with now rather than be stuck when you get upstairs[2]?"

"But let's say the *Dayonim* get it wrong themselves?" objected Uzi. "Then I'll really be messed up and for no good reason either."

"Why should the *Dayonim* get it wrong?" challenged Chanoch. "It's their job to search out the truth and they have more than enough experience to see through any trickster's façade."

"I'm still not sure," said Uzi nervously. "You hear so many stories nowadays about *Dayonim* being bribed and messing up, why would *anyone* want to subject themselves to such a corrupt system?"

Chanoch had to laugh at this inane objection.

---

2. colloquial expression used to refer to one's situation after death

"Of course there are vicious rumors circulating," he guffawed. "Do you know who circulates them? All the sore losers! Rather than gracefully acknowledge defeat they would rather badmouth the proficiency of the *Dayonim*. Criminal if you ask me but what can you do? And I don't believe for one second that civil courts are even half as good either," he added, wagging an angry finger in the air.

Despite Chanoch's convincing arguments, Uzi remained carefully guarded against trying to settle his argument with the Benarroches in a Din Torah. However, when *they* took the initiative and presented *him* with an ultimatum to attend a Beis Din, there really was no choice but to accede to the request.

ઙ ઙ ઙ

It was to be the longest day. Poised for battle, Uzi sat in the courtroom fully alert and ready to tackle the Benarroches. He had spent considerable time amassing the relevant documents, organizing his defense and also preparing some counterclaims of his own. The plush leather armchair made him feel quite at home and he gazed across the magnificent oak desk before him, up to the bench where the *Dayonim* were seated. That was his first disconcerting moment. Despite what Chanoch had told him, they looked particularly severe, their long white beards flowing hauntingly over impeccably-pressed black caftans as they peered at him coldly through horn-rimmed spectacles.

Meanwhile, on a parallel table sat Chaim Benarroch who seemed content to let his wife Chaya do all the talking. And talk she did. In vivid detail she began describing the awful mess Uzi and his builders had created, detailing every last complaint imaginable. Chaim sat quietly as she spoke, merely smiling in a nauseating way every time she aired a different grievance.

"And this entire mess was only because of the complete and total incompetence of YOU!" she burst out loudly, turning from the *Dayonim* to face off against Uzi personally.

"YOU MADE PROMISES PROMISES PROMISES!" she yelled, "AND THEY WERE ALL *LIES*!" she screamed louder, leaping out of her seat. The force of the movement sent her chair flying to the ground but she seemed oblivious as she stood up to full height, inhaling deeply. With cheeks blazing red and fire burning in her eyes, she grasped the fallen chair with one hand and slowly and deliberately began marching across the courtroom until she was standing menacingly in front of Uzi's table.

"You tore our house to shreds, rent our family asunder and still have the gall to just sit there and STARE!"

Chaim looked utterly shocked at his wife's outburst yet seemed frozen in his seat, powerless to intervene. Uzi looked helplessly towards the *Dayonim* but they seemed to be actually enjoying the scene, contentedly watching justice take its course. Uzi shrank back but there was no avoiding the fury burning from the anger-filled nostrils of his accuser. In horror, he watched as she raised the chair high into the air, pausing only for a second before bringing it down towards him with all her energy and pent-up anger.

"AAAAAARRRGGGGGHHHHHHH!" screamed Uzi as he felt himself falling to the floor.

"Uzi, *Ma zeh imcha,?*" asked his wife groggily, referencing the alarm clock next to her bed. "Is everything okay with you? Why are you lying on the floor and making such a noise at four o'clock in the morning?"

"Benarroch!" he managed to whine between desperate gasps. "It was her again, coming to exact revenge. AVIVA! I JUST CAN'T TAKE THIS ANYMORE. Why do these people have to take me to Din Torah? I never meant to harm them or anything."

"Uzi, take it easy," coaxed Aviva encouragingly. "Your friend said all would be fine and you should just listen to him and stop harassing yourself with all this paranoia. Now go back to sleep and try to stop thinking about it."

"Okay, I suppose you're right," replied Uzi as he climbed onto the bed and laid his head back down upon the sweat-soaked pillow.

☙ ☙ ☙

It was an ironic case of role reversal. Knowing her husband was spending the day in Beis Din, a tense, almost paranoid Aviva had made every precaution to ensure a relaxing and therapeutic end to his day. A carefully balanced meal lay waiting, each course cooked to perfection and just at the correct temperature, giving no room for further upset. A pot of freshly brewed coffee and a pecan pie lay waiting for Uzi and there was even a full glass of arak[3] standing by to offset any possible adverse reaction to the day's events.

---

3. aniseed liqueur

Hearing his truck pulling up outside signaled to Aviva her ordeal was about to begin and, inhaling deeply she braced herself and opened the front door to greet him.

"You know Aviva, you were right after all," she heard him say calmly as he ascended the front step. "There really was nothing to be scared of after all. Everything happened just as Chanoch had predicted. Say, what's this pecan pie doing here Vivi?" he asked suddenly spying his favorite delicacy on the table, "and why are you looking so tense?"

No explanation would have sufficed to describe how Aviva had spent the day and instead she listened kindly as he described to her the afternoon's events.

"When I first arrived in the Beis Din building it was the weirdest thing. I almost crashed into Mr. Benarroch when he was parking his car in the narrow lot but aside from that everything went very smoothly. In the reception area we were met by this short, cute, stocky guy with a huge smile who actually turned out to be that Rabbi Salzman who had spoken to us on the phone before. He calls himself the *safreh d'dayna* but that's just really a scary name for court secretary. Anyhow, he started by introducing himself and then explained exactly how the Din Torah was to take place so we would know what to do, and when to speak and so on.

It got a bit scary when he took us into the courtroom but it turned out that the three *Dayonim* on the case were nothing at all like the guys I kept on dreaming about."

"Really!" commented Aviva, her state of mind slowly switching from one of concern to that of genuine interest.

"Only one of them had a white beard and he looked like a friendly version of our Rabbi Barkany and not at all scary. The middle one had a red beard and he spoke with such an accent he must be European or something. He couldn't even say 'th' properly and it took a while to get used to it and understand him. The third guy, I mean *Dayan* was this tall brain box type who didn't say very much to us, but kept whispering things to the older guy."

"So what happened then?" asked Aviva. "How did the arguing go?"

"That was the funny thing. There wasn't even so much arguing. The first thing they asked us was if we wanted *Din* or *pshoro*. Chanoch had warned me they would and advised to agree to a *pshoro* but Mr. Benarroch wasn't so sure and it took Rabbi Salzman a lot of explaining to convince him that it would be a much quicker and easier way to settle the case. Then Benarroch got to speak first and started by pulling out our contract. Well I couldn't exactly argue with that. It did say clearly that I would have to pay him two thousand dollars a month if I finished late, and he also wanted money because his daughters had to rent a different place for their day camp because the yard was still a mess and we hadn't finished with the trucks in time."

"So you agreed to pay then?" asked Aviva worriedly.

"No," said Uzi, "or not exactly anyway. I told them that it's true that I signed but I had no idea it would take so long to finish the job and also, most of the things that caused the delay weren't even my fault."

"Is that enough of a reason for you not to have to pay?"

"I don't know, but it's the truth and I wasn't exactly going to start lying to the *Dayonim*. But the next thing went better. He complained that I kept on jacking up the price and was really stealing from him by going above my original estimate. So I just opened the file and took out all the receipts proving that everything had cost more than I thought when I first gave him a price. He didn't believe me but I told him that lumber had nearly doubled in price in the past year and it wasn't fair for him to blame me for not knowing the price was going to go up."

"So what happened next?"

"Then he came with a whole list of things that hadn't been finished yet and that it wasn't right how I had left the job in the middle without finishing up. Very funny! I told the *Dayonim* that I wasn't going to work if he wasn't going to pay me and that's why I kept away. I told them that I would be quite happy to go and finish up once the money thing was sorted out, but he said he'd had enough and just wanted money back instead."

"Are you sure you want to do that? Like go back to his house and do more work?"

"Why not? It'll be a lot cheaper than having him hire someone else and then send me the bill. Anyhow, that'll be up to the *Dayonim* to decide."

"What else did Benarroch say?"

"That was basically all. After that the *Dayan* with the red beard summed up what had been said to make sure they had understood it all correctly. He did quite a good job and apart from one or two things that Benarroch wanted clarified there wasn't much else to say. Then the *Dayonim* stood up and left the room. After they'd gone Rabbi Salzman told us we'd probably receive a ruling in about two weeks and we should call him as soon as possible in case there was a problem. Then it was over and he let us go home."

ᘓ ᘓ ᘓ

Despite his positive Beis Din experience, Uzi remained cautiously guarded over how the case would be resolved, his trauma from previous nights only slightly diminished. Then, one morning, about ten days later the letter arrived. From the outside it looked innocent enough, just an unpretentious, white envelope with the Beis Din's name and address printed in the upper left hand corner. But Uzi knew full well this plain façade belied the importance and gravity of its contents. In fact, maybe this was all part of the Beis Din's evil and insidious plan? Maybe they were trying to lull him into a false sense of security, only to shatter it with the violent coupe-de-grace of an adverse judgment? Agonizingly, he opened the envelope, took out the letter and unfolded it.

The two lines of printed text were brief, succinct and to the point. Uzi read them once, and then again before deciding there was no negative inferences in the simple letter.

"Vivi, look at this," he finally called out enthusiastically to his wife. "The Beis Din must have liked my story after all! I've just got to finish the work like I wanted to and apart from a five hundred dollar deduction Benarroch has to pay in full."

Aviva beamed back at the good news, suggesting a celebratory *l'chaim* to which Uzi happily agreed.

Meanwhile, at the Benarroch residence, Chaim wasn't faring so well.

"What do you mean you agreed to a *pshoro*?" said a horrified Chaya Benarroch in response to her husband's feeble explanation of the meaning of the letter. "I thought we agreed you were going to take that Uzi to the cleaners and get every last penny from him for messing us around."

"I know, but it's just that he looked so sorry and pitiful in the Beis Din and maybe it wasn't even all his fault, I thought it was only fair to agree to a *pshoro* with him. Believe me, he looked quite different in a suit and tie that he normally does in those awful overalls."

"Well you must have goofed up big time on the arguments then," reasoned Chaya more vociferously. "Why else would we have lost so badly!"

"No, I didn't," stressed Chaim in return. "I told them everything and they even repeated it back to show they had understood it all. There just must be another explanation. Maybe Rabbi Salzman can explain it to me?"

Chaya however, her cheeks blazing red and fire flashing in her eyes did not seem too interested at that point in listening to any explanation Rabbi Salzman could have offered.

"Maybe a small after-breakfast arak then instead?" Chaim weakly offered.

☞ *Would Chaim have fared better in the Din Torah had he not agreed to pshoro-compromise and insisted on strict Din instead?* *(p. 217)*

4

Impounded

Life could hardly have been more perfect for Benzy and Shani Silver. After a wonderful wedding they had spent a blissful few months settling down together in their new home and were now getting ready for a greatly anticipated summer vacation in Israel. The suitcases were neatly packed, their passports in order and a friendly neighbor had even kindly agreed to look after the mail. Sitting back together in a new car they prepared for a relaxed journey to the airport.

"What a beautiful day for traveling," remarked Shani. "And everything's gone so smoothly."

"Right," agreed Benzy. "Even Mr. Warrens and Fido seemed in a good mood," he added referring to their less-than-friendly neighbor, "and that beats everything."

"Maybe he was just glad to see the back of us for a while," reasoned Shani. "He's always complaining that the block's become too busy for him in his old age and how much he misses the days when he could just enjoy a quiet life."

"I just can't understand why he doesn't simply move out like the rest of his cronies did. He's so moody and bad-tempered he'd do everyone a favor by packing out for good!"

Thankfully, thoughts of Mr. Warrens and his mean dog were soon forgotten as Benzy and Shani's airplane took to the skies, leaving all souring thoughts behind. A pleasant flight and smooth landing sufficed to put them further at ease, allowing them to enjoy to the fullest their ambitious touring schedule.

They traveled from the hot, sunny Mediterranean beaches up to the elevating, spiritual peaks of the mountainous Tzfas region, every minute proving to be most fulfilling and worthwhile.

With their arrival in Jerusalem for the final days before their scheduled return, the trip began to assume a more personal tone for Benzy as he began to relive the days he had spent as a teenage student in the city. With boyish enthusiasm he trekked Shani up and down the cobbled streets of Meah Shearim pointing out various places of minimal interest to all but the initiated.

"Do you think we could take a break now?" she asked him weakly at one point. "I think I could use a rest."

"Me too!" agreed Benzy. "In fact," he continued excitedly, "The perfect place for lunch is coming up just around the next corner!"

With that said, he led her down another alley until they were standing outside something vaguely resembling a pizzeria. Following her husband, Shani entered the dimly lit store, walked down the narrow staircase and settled down at a table while Benzy brought the pizza. While he munched hungrily Shani ate sparingly, casting disdainful looks at their less than hygienic surroundings.

"Life must have been tough for you in yeshiva," she finally commented. "Having to survive these rickety steps, this greasy food and the germs all over this place!"

"Yeah!" replied Benzy, chomping heartily. "Real *mesiras nefesh* for *Torah*."

These noble epithets were soon interrupted by a cry of recognition from a table across the aisle.

"Benzy and Shani is that you?" cried the voice.

"Moshe Dovid!" exclaimed Shani upon seeing her nephew. "Don't tell me you also have the misfortune to frequent this seedy place!" she joked politely, pityingly eyeing his pizza-bedecked lunch tray. "Is there nowhere else in town you can find something to eat?"

"Shani, please!" Benzy cajoled her. "Peretz's Pizza Parlor is famous all over Jerusalem and a great place to meet people! Here Moshe Dovid," he said turning to his friend and now nephew. "Pull up a chair and sit next to us!"

Moshe Dovid obliged and listened politely as Benzy regaled him with an array of wondrous tales from their experiences of the previous two weeks.

"We've only got four days left until we leave," Benzy finally commented, "but I'm sure it'll be enough to fit in everything I still want to do."

"Four days?" repeated Moshe Dovid thoughtfully. "You're leaving on Monday then?"

"Yeah, sort of. I think our flight actually leaves shortly after midnight which is really first thing Tuesday morning."

"Hey, that's cool! I'm also flying then," exclaimed Moshe Dovid excitedly. "Any idea how you're getting to the airport? It'd be great if we could share a taxi."

"Sounds good," replied Benzy. "Give us a call on Monday morning and we'll arrange it then."

ન ન ન

It was an emotional *Shacharis* for Moshe Dovid that following Monday morning. Sunrise at the *Kossel* had been an obvious choice and with such an early start he had already breakfasted and completed his packing by eleven o'clock. All that remained was to arrange a taxi to the airport but alas Moshe Dovid found his calls to the Silver's hotel room inexplicably unanswered. After half an hour of fruitless trying he took to the streets and headed out for Eizenbach's Hotel to investigate for himself.

Predictably, the hotel receptionist was as unhelpful in person as she had been on the phone. Reluctant to divulge the whereabouts of the Silver's room she merely directed Moshe Dovid to a small table situated in a distant corner upon which sat the rather ancient-looking house phone. Once again however, there was no reply from the room.

"Are you sure you've given me the correct number?" he asked upon returning to the reception desk. "I'm not getting any reply from their room and they did tell me they would be here now."

"You have been given the correct number sir and if my guests choose to ignore your persistent calls then that is their prerogative," she maintained strictly. "At this point it might be more appropriate for you to leave the premises since your party seems to be unavailable."

Given this not illogical ultimatum Moshe Dovid resigned himself to arranging alternative airport transportation, gradually making his way towards the hotel exit. As he approached the door, a taxi pulled up right in front of him and from out of the passenger seat stepped a tired looking Benzy Silver.

"Benzy, here you are!" exclaimed Moshe Dovid, quite shocked at finding his mission's quest so providentially fulfilled. "Where have you been all morning? I tried reaching you but there was no reply in your room."

"Makes sense," replied Benzy flatly as he turned and opened the rear passenger door. There, seated across the entire rear bench sat Shani her right foot bandaged in a huge plaster cast. "Now you see why we weren't in this morning?" continued Benzy. "We've just spent the past twelve hours in the hospital emergency room."

This explanation more than sufficed to silence Moshe Dovid and, trying to appear helpful, he escorted Benzy and the crutch-ridden Shani into the hotel. The receptionist appeared only mildly startled upon seeing this strange threesome enter, not interfering as they made their way across the lobby to the elevators.

Tactfully, Moshe Dovid waited downstairs while Benzy took his wife into the elevator and up to their room. Ten minutes later Benzy reappeared to face a barrage of questions from a most curious, inquisitive and concerned Moshe Dovid

"What's going on? What on earth happened?" he blurted out. "What happened to Shani?"

"Moshe Dovid, you don't even *want* to know," replied Benzy despondently. "We were getting off a bus late last night when she slipped and fell on the sidewalk. She couldn't walk at all so we took a taxi straight to the hospital emergency room. It took hours to get x-rays taken and have a doctor look at her, but eventually they decided she's broken her ankle and is going to need surgery to set it back correctly."

"Oh no, that's awful!" exclaimed Moshe Dovid. "How terrible for her! Are…are you still planning on making the flight this evening? I mean…… do you think your wife will be okay flying with her leg plastered up like that?"

"Are you kidding?!" replied Benzy. "I don't think she'd even make it as far as the airport with her leg, never mind flying!" This obviously put paid to Moshe Dovid's money-saving, shared-taxi scheme but despite this upset his main concern was with his aunt's plainly more difficult plight.

"Is there at least anything I can do to help you now?" he kindly offered. "I know there's only a few hours remaining before I have to go to the airport but if there's anything I can do before then just ask."

"You know," replied Benzy thoughtfully, "maybe there is actually something you could do for us but back home, not here. Before we left we parked our car in a hotel near the airport but I only prepaid the parking until tomorrow morning. I was going to call the hotel to tell them we got delayed so they won't tow it away but it'd be a lot better if you could just pick it up for us and drive it home instead."

"For sure I'll do that for you," replied Moshe Dovid enthusiastically. "It'll also save me trying to hitch or take a taxi home."

"Good, excellent," sighed Benzy. "At least that's one problem out of the way. Let me give you all the details to make sure you can find it alright."

Moshe Dovid listened carefully as Benzy described exactly where the car was located and what it looked like.

"They've actually kept the key there in case they've needed to move it while we've been away, but if you just give them this receipt and some identification it'll be no problem. And when you get home just park the car by my house. The spot's right outside and you shouldn't have any trouble finding it."

With this, Benzy bid Moshe Dovid farewell and good luck with the car quest before excusing himself to return and tend to his injured wife.

☙ ☙ ☙

It wasn't exactly a lightning cure, but the surgery on Shani's broken ankle was deemed by the doctors successful enough to allow her to fly home after twenty four hours, a mere seven days after the original accident. The packing and preparations fell to Benzy but the burden of these chores paled in comparison to Shani's ordeal in getting home. Spending twelve hours in the confines of an airplane trying to keep her leg elevated gave her more than enough to cope with and the bumpy ride home from the airport was even worse. Her harrowing ordeal finally came to its end when their taxi pulled up in front of their home parking squarely opposite the front door.

Shani hobbled out on her crutches and up the front step followed by Benzy and then the driver with the luggage. Eager for a generous tip, the driver ensured to point out his prowess in selecting a prime parking position.

"Good that I managed to park right by your front door, wasn't it sir,' he commented. "Easy for the misses to get home, right guv?"

"Oh yes! I guess it was," replied Benzy dimly, notably more concerned at that point with his wife. Then, as the driver's words slowly penetrated, it dawned upon Benzy that something was perhaps amiss.

"Shani, what do you think Moshe Dovid has done with our car?" he asked worriedly. "He was meant to have parked it right here but I don't see it anywhere. I hope he didn't forget and left it at the airport!"

Given her temporary disablement and immediate comfort requirements Shani was not in a position to concern herself with such trivialities as a missing car.

"Benzy, I don't know and I don't care either. If you can't find it just go and buy another one!"

Correcting his priorities Benzy quickly paid and dismissed the driver, then turned to the eminently more important task of caring for Shani. It took quite some time to settle her back comfortably in their home, and only after this had been successfully achieved did he dare venture out in search of the car.

Tracking down his wife's nephew proved simple enough but unfortunately Moshe Dovid was unable to shed any light on the whereabouts of the missing car.

"I just parked it outside of your house like we arranged," he insisted, "and I even made sure to lock all the doors before I left it."

"But that just doesn't make sense," insisted Benzy. "The car certainly isn't there anymore. Do you still have the key? Maybe someone got a hold of it and has borrowed the car without us knowing."

"I don't think so," replied Moshe Dovid reaching into his pocket. "I put it onto my key ring as soon as you gave it to me and it hasn't been moved from there since."

Benzy inspected Moshe Dovid's proffered key fob and sure enough, the car key was right there.

"This is really confusing," said Benzy. "Are you sure you parked it outside our house?" he pressed further. "Maybe you got the number wrong or parked it on a different block?"

"I…I don't think so," said Moshe Dovid worriedly. "It was one four seven Archibald Terrace right? A brown house with a yellow front door?"

"Yes, you're correct. That does sound like our house," confirmed Benzy. "I just don't get it then. Where could our car be? I hope it hasn't been stolen or something."

"I hope not too," commiserated Moshe Dovid anxiously.

However, without any other viable alternatives to consider, the stolen theory did seem to be the most likely. After returning home empty handed, a dejected Benzy contacted the local police to inform them of the loss. However, while sounding sympathetic, the receptionist was unwilling to process the information or take any action until official protocol had been followed.

"I'm sorry sir but we can't take a report for a stolen vehicle over the telephone," she explained patiently. "We'll need to send an officer over to conduct a face-to-face interview. Now, where did you say you lived?"

Benzy provided all the relevant details and was calmly assured that a police detective would visit them at home later that day.

While this news may have been a first positive step to recovering the car, Shani was less than thrilled at the prospect of a police visit to their home, especially in its present disorderly state. Gallantly, Benzy made a bold effort to compensate for his wife's inability to clean, rising quickly to stash the suitcases out of the way but no sooner had he begun did a squad car pull up, right outside their front door.

"I say officer, that was fast," said a flustered Benzy as he opened up for this important visitor. "We didn't think you'd be here that quickly."

Officer Macdonald smiled broadly, his pride at this achievement exceedingly apparently.

"Oh, that's fine sir, just part of the job," he replied dismissively. "I was actually on this block a few days ago, so when your call came in finding you was really easy. Now, what seems to be the trouble today?" he asked seating himself down at the dining room table.

“I’m afraid to say that we think our car’s been stolen,” Benzy blurted out in hurried confusion. “We just came back from vacation and my friend drove it back from the airport and although he said he left it here once he’d finished the drive, when we came back today it was gone and he says that he’s sure it was left where it was meant to be and he even gave me back the key so he for sure doesn’t have it anymore.”

With all the airs of the seasoned professional Officer Macdonald inhaled deeply after Benzy had ended his convolution just to confirm that he had indeed finished.

“Okay sir do you think we could perhaps take this one stage at a time,” he requested extracting a notepad from the breast pocket on his uniform. “Now, you say your car’s been stolen, correct?”

“Yes sir.”

“Year, make, model and license plate?”

“It’s a two thousand and eight Fiat Helix, license MNS 461.”

The officer wrinkled his nose thoughtfully at this information before writing it down in his book.

“Okay good. Now, where was the vehicle last seen?”

“Just outside our house. My friend parked it there last week and now it’s gone.”

Officer Macdonald began writing again and then paused as if struggling to digest the information he was being given.

“Who did you say parked the car?”

"My friend. He drove it back from the airport for us because my wife broke her ankle and we couldn't come back when we had wanted to."

"Do you know *exactly* where your friend parked the car?" asked the officer more insistently. "Perhaps we should be having a word with him to confirm the precise details of the story?"

Benzy was quite confused by the officer's line of questioning and tried to reassure him that Moshe Dovid had done nothing illegal.

"That may well be sir," continued Macdonald, "but I think I may be able to solve this crime faster than you think."

With those words the officer retreated outside and began talking rapidly into his radio leaving a puzzled Benzy and Shani waiting inside. It didn't take more than a few minutes before Macdonald returned.

"I have good news for you sir," he said, a big smile spread across his face. "We've found your car."

"What!" exclaimed Benzy. "You've found my car already? Well that's fantastic! Is…is it still in one piece?"

"Absolutely! It's being well cared for in our tow pound," explained the officer. "Now if you'd care to come down to the station and complete some paperwork we'll be glad to release the vehicle to you just as soon as you'd like. I can even give you a ride there right now if you'd wish."

Benzy was delighted with this quick development and excitedly made his way to station headquarters to retrieve the car. However, when he arrived there was some unpleasant news awaiting him.

"I'm glad you've come to retrieve your car sir," the receptionist informed him. "Police charges for impounding and storing the vehicle add up to four hundred and twenty dollars. Will you be paying cash or check?"

"WHHAAAAATT!" exclaimed Benzy. "How much money did you say you wanted?"

"Four hundred and twenty dollars."

"B...b…b…but what for?" asked Benzy. "It's not my fault that someone stole my car."

The receptionist looked towards officer Macdonald who was only too happy to explain.

"Sir, your vehicle was never stolen," he explained. "The problem was illegal parking. Last week we received a call from your neighbor, one Mr. Warrens that the vehicle was illegally parked in his spot and we had no option but to come and tow it away."

"You mean……….."

"Exactly sir! Your friend parked it in the wrong spot, actually one space too far to the right. Sorry about that. Maybe next time he should be more careful."

☞ *Is Moshe Dovid responsible for the police towing and impounding fees? (p. 221)*

5

Squirrels

It was Norman Strauss's worst nightmare come true. The epitome of suburban servitude, it had always been his self-appointed task to maintain his home in pristine, flawless condition. The windows were forever sparkling clean, the bushes constantly trimmed to a neat precision and the lawn most certainly kept to its manicured perfection. However, some recent sciuridaean activity in the immediate vicinity threatened to undermine the very foundations of this pristine, urbane existence.

"NORMAN! THEY'VE DONE IT AGAIN!" shrieked Sybil Strauss glancing out the front room window. "This time they've left the remains of yesterday's supper all over the grass, and there's also some newspapers and an old tuna-fish can. Norman, this is so embarrassing! Now the neighbors will see we don't buy the national brand!"

Norman tore himself from a morning coffee to be at Sybil's side and together they gazed out at the harrowing sight of their litter-strewn front lawn. Even as they stood watching, another small, furry, gray-bodied rodent appeared from underneath a rhododendron bush at the edge of their property. Twitching its head sharply from side to side, it paused before darting across the lawn straight towards the garbage area. Incredible as it seemed the creature then squeezed itself through a hole seemingly far too small to accommodate its fattened body before disappearing into the bosoms of the closest garbage can.

"Norman! Do something NOW!" insisted Sybil prompting her husband to venture outside into the garden. Bravely he made his way towards where the can stood, holding the kitchen broom out in front of him. Two sharp bangs on the side sufficed to stir the squirrel from its forage and it quickly emerged from the hole and zipped off into the distance.

With the ravaging rodent now gone Norman contented himself with clearing off the garbage from the lawn but it was clear that a more permanent solution to the pest problem was needed. How exactly to deal with the issue was the conjecture of many of his colleagues at work in the following days.

"Have you tried setting traps for them? That generally helps."

"I find ammonia in the garbage keeps them at bay?"

"Double wrap all food waste so they won't be able to smell it."

"Nuke 'em out, it's the only way."

Some of the suggestions were more practical than others. But it was Sam Finkelstein's idea that rang the truest.

"Find out where they nest and then destroy their lair," he suggested. "Then they'll simply go somewhere else and leave you alone. It shouldn't be too hard to do if you watch them closely enough."

Heeding this advice, Norman began paying closer attention to the movements of the bothersome beasts and soon observed how they seemed to center their movements around the large oak tree that stood adjacent to the side of the house. The creatures would run across the yard, up into the tree and then disappear from sight. Sometimes they would reappear on a branch higher up but exactly where in the tree they resided still remained a mystery.

Finally, one quiet evening when all was still at home, that question too received its answer. Norman had been lying awake quite harmlessly in his bed when a faint but distinct scratching noise echoed quietly through his bedroom. Straining to locate the source of the sound Norman found himself looking upwards towards the ceiling and slowly the realization of where the squirrels were roosting dawned upon him. Horror of horrors, the vermin were living in his very own attic!

ᏄᏄᏄ

"They've obviously found a hole somewhere or burrowed through one of the soffits near the tree," explained Sam upon hearing of the unfortunate discovery. "Shouldn't be too hard to fix. Call down someone to patch the hole and that should solve the problem."

Taking his friend's advice to the next stage, Norman called down Rafi's Roofs Inc. to fix the problem. With polite efficiency, Rafi was soon at the Strauss home investigating the possibility of a hole or access point for the pests. First using binoculars and then a ladder he had soon pinpointed exactly where the problem lay.

"Yup, there is a small hole here underneath the eaves just on top of the gutters," explained Rafi. "Shouldn't take too long to fix up and patch, and the price would be three hundred dollars. Is that okay?"

Rafi's confident manner fairly convinced Sybil of the argument for instant action, but Norman remained cautiously guarded.

"But supposing you close up the hole," he asked, "and the squirrels are still home. Then what will happen?"

"That would be *terrible*!" confirmed Rafi, "They'd go berserk like caged animals, but not if we do the job now when they'll be out foraging for food. It's only later in the day and early evening that they start coming home. But just wait until they do. When they see how well I've sealed up this hole.... well then they'll just go off and search for some other place to live instead," he guffawed, laughing unpleasantly.

"Okay if you say so," said Norman. "Just make sure you seal up that hole properly and make sure there are no others either."

Rafi confidently assured Norman all would be well and proceeded back to his truck to locate the correct tools and materials for the job.

It was obvious from the way he worked that Rafi was a man who knew his trade well. First he cut a wooden patch to size and when that had been screwed in place he proceeded to cover it with layer upon layer of different protective coatings to keep both the squirrels and the weather at bay. Finally, after an hour and a half the job had been completed and Rafi descended the ladder, a smile of satisfaction on his face.

"Now sir you have nothing to worry about," he told Norman confidently. "My repair will keep out even the most determined of squirrels!"

That night Norman went to bed a happy man. He could now sleep in peace the cleanliness of his morning lawn again reassured. However, no sooner had he drifted off into a horticultured dreamland was his sleep most disturbingly disrupted. This time it wasn't necessary to carefully listen out for the source of the sound. The wild scampering that could be heard from above more than aptly demonstrated exactly what the problem was and from where it was coming. Sybil too had heard the noises and she sat up and looked worriedly at her husband.

"You don't suppose those squirrels have found their way back in again Norman, do you?" she asked worriedly.

"Worse than that!" he cried back drowning out the sounds of the desperate creatures. "They never escaped in the first place! That lunatic of a roofer must have left them inside when he closed up that hole."

"Oh dear!" exclaimed Sybil. "What are we going to do now?"

"There's nothing else for it," said Norman determinedly. "This time we'll have to call a professional and have him deal with the problem properly."

It was Eric the Exterminator who was the fortunate recipient of the Strauss's next call and he scheduled to meet with them later that same day. Arriving on the scene, he listened carefully to Norman and Sybil before agreeing wholeheartedly with their bitter diagnosis.

"I see this the whole time," Eric explained. "These cowboys come along, think they know it all and just patch up the hole as if that'll solve the problem. But it's just not that simple. You've first got to give the squirrels warning to get out and only then seal it up afterwards. Watch carefully and you'll see what I mean."

Eric then fetched his own ladder and ascended up to where Rafi had worked the previous day. Gingerly, he began removing the caulk, the shingles and all the other roofing materials Rafi had used until the naked wooden patch was revealed before him. Making sure his footing was sure on the ladder, Eric then began removing the screws holding the patch in place. First came one screw, then the next, then the third and at last he was ready for the final screw.

"OKAY, HERE WE GO!" he yelled down to the group of neighbors who had gathered below to watch the spectacle. "JUST WATCH THEM DARNED CRITTERS GO!" and no sooner had he removed that last screw did four squirrels fly out of the roof like lightning, scrambling down the tree and dashing off across the yard towards the seclusion of a small cluster of bushes further down the block.

"Yes sirree," announced Eric triumphantly. "You can be sure there ain't no more squirrels in that there attic no more, I guarantee it," and with that began to repatch the hole precluding entry to any other would-be intruders.

With the job completed Eric descended his ladder and presented the Strausses with his final bill.

"Yes sirree, that'll be three hundred dollars for the job if you please and I'm glad to have been of service to you today."

Norman shrugged his shoulders in Sybil's direction and begrudgingly paid Eric his requested fee without protest. For it was the roofer, Rafi who was to be on the receiving end of Norman's wrath.

"Do you realize I gave you three hundred dollars for NOTHING!" he complained angrily into the phone much to the roofer's distaste. "All you did was seal up the hole so well there was no way the squirrels inside could escape and it cost me another three hundred dollars to fix the problem."

"Listen sir, you can hardly blame me," countered Rafi, attempting to justify his position. "I'm only a roofer not an exterminator and I gave you the best information and advice I could based on my experience. You hired me to fix a hole in your roof which I certainly did most professionally and any extermination work I was meant to be doing was nothing to do with my fee anyway. So if you're expecting a refund, FORGET IT!"

☞ *Is Norman entitled to a refund from Rafi for not doing the job properly?* *(p. 224)*

6

Fate and Fortune

To most people the onset of unfavorable weather is akin to a downturn in the market or a nagging toothache. The day is dulled, one's energy sapped and hopes for a better tomorrow abound. Warren Maccallister though was not most people. After youthful successes as an umbrella distributor, Warren discovered an amazing correlation between inclement weather and the sweeping success of bumper sales in his second career. Apparently, the incidence of gray, dull, overcast skies and even better, rains weeping from the heavens made potential customers invariably more receptive to the power of his message. Thus, it was with a happy heart he took note of the oncoming storm clouds as he approached the door of his next target, one Feitl Groner.

Had Warren known Feitl better he could just as well have exulted in the warm beauty of a sun-filled sky. Blessed with a free hand, a concerned and listening heart and an erratic but ready supply of cash Feitl was a more-than-likely candidate for favorably receiving Warren's sales pitch. In fact their entire meeting lasted little more than half-an-hour by which time Warren had secured the business of yet another lucrative client.

Much to his surprise though, a request for consideration for his services met with a most unexpected response. Whereas most of his customers would simply write out a check, Feitl instead seemed determined to pay in cash, and Warren watched in amazement as wad after wad of crumpled bills emerged out of Feitl's pockets to be placed onto the dining room table before them. It took Warren several minutes to count the growing pile of bills but eventually he was satisfied the required total had been reached.

"To be honest," quipped the salesman as he made to exit, "I hadn't really expected a cash payment. However if you do prefer currency it'll be my pleasure to continue servicing you personally in the future."

"Just make sure you bring a big envelope with you next time," chuckled Feitl in response. "I wouldn't want your suit pockets to end up bursting like mine always do!"

☙ ☙ ☙

Reuven Groner would remember the day well. It had started as any other but took an adverse turn mid-morning with his wife's urgent phone call to the office.

"It's your father!" she said quickly. "I just got a call that he collapsed on his way home from *shul* and was rushed into Falkirk Medical. You've got to go right now and see what's going on there."

While swift and sobering, news of the collapse could hardly have been dubbed surprising. Living alone, Reuven's father lived a haphazard and unstructured lifestyle which, combined with previous health issues and a sizable weight problem, left him more than a likely candidate for the sudden attack that had robbed him of his consciousness. Now, standing by the hospital bedside, Reuven listened worriedly as Dr. Dumenglume invoked those same reasons in giving his cheerless synopsis of the unfortunate Feitl's situation.

"I'm afraid Mr. Groner that it appears your father has suffered a major stroke," he said gravely. "Our initial brain scan indicates a lack of blood to forward parts of the cerebrum. How severely this has affected him will remain a mystery until he awakens and while some victims can make an almost complete recovery others can.......... well let's not discuss that until we need to."

While the grimness of prediction had been left unuttered, Feitl's recovery seemed destined to follow an ill-fortuned path nonetheless. Consciousness was not quick to return and often he seemed more with the dead than with the living. Even when his eyelids did flutter open it was only for brief periods and he remained no more than semi-conscious for any extended period of time.

During this difficult period of uncertainty Reuven had undertaken the task of attending to his father's personal and financial affairs. This transpired to be a thoroughly impossible task for with little or no track of how Feitl managed his finances, every day brought new twists and surprises. Unexplained bills and demands for payments kept Reuven constantly busy explaining to the myriad of creditors his father's condition and how payment would have to wait.

One evening while he was at the family home fending off the phone company from cutting service there was a loud, confident knocking at the door. Cautious of another mysterious business acquaintance, Reuven made good use of the door peephole spying out an impeccably dressed, bareheaded, friendly, almost harmless looking middle-aged, gentleman. Only slightly prematurely the man knocked again prompting Reuven to open the door.

"Yes? Is there something I can help you with?" he asked curiously.

"I was wondering if I may speak with Mr. Groner please," replied a rigidly polite Warren Maccallister, disguising any notion of surprise he may have had that Feitl himself had not opened the door.

"I'm afraid Mr. Groner is not in at present. Is there perhaps something *I* could help you with?"

Warren was ready to politely excuse himself and return later but something about Reuven's self-assured confidence made the salesman rethink this strategy.

"Possibly," he finally said. "Are you sir perhaps one Reuben Groner?"

Hearing his name articulated by a total stranger gave Reuven reason enough to greater consider this mysterious individual and he nodded in silent confirmation.

"Perhaps it would be appropriate then sir if I could have a word with you instead?" asked Warren motioning as if to enter the home.

This request was not denied and, mimicking the actions of an authentic homeowner Reuven showed Warren into the dining room. However, such direction was seemingly unnecessary as Warren's knowledge of the house's interior clearly indicated he had been there before.

"You know my father?" Reuven said, more as a statement of fact than a question.

"Yes I do," replied Warren. "Is everything okay? It isn't like him not to be home when I call."

Delicately, Reuven explained his father's situation and how the elder Mr. Groner was essentially out of commission until further notice.

"I have assumed charge over his most pressing affairs," Reuven concluded, "but for anything else I would suggest you call back in a few months when hopefully he will have recovered somewhat and be more accessible."

Reuven had hoped this explanation would suffice in dismissing Warren but it seemed to evoke a precisely opposite reaction from the salesman

"Mr. Groner, I assure you my business here today is of most pressing a manner indeed and requiring of your immediate attention," countered Warren. "In fact, even more so than I had first thought just a very short while ago. If I may trouble you, can I suggest you peruse through this letter and digest its contests?"

Reuven observed for a moment the folio of excellent quality Warren proffered before accepting it into his own hand. Although not addressed to Reuven personally, the gravity and importance of its message had strong personal ramifications indeed. And, as Warren had inferred, its contents were of an extremely timely nature.

Dear Mr. Groner,

We have not received this year's premiums for your $1,000,000 term-life insurance policy #3576032J. Please be advised that if your payment of $16,878.46 is not received within seven days from the date of this letter your policy will automatically cancel and not be renewable.

Please disregard this letter if payment has already been made.

Yours sincerely,

Warren Maccallister, Policy Manager.

After reading the letter twice Reuven raised his eyes in question towards its bearer.

"And you sir are…..?" asked Reuven.

"Warren Maccallister."

"I thought as much," mused Reuven, his brow furrowed in thought. "Can you please explain to me exactly what this is all about?"

"Certainly Mr. Groner," began the salesman. "Approximately nine years ago I first called upon your father and introduced him to the idea of life insurance, something he had never previously considered. We briefly ran through the highlights of some of the products our company had to offer and almost without hesitation he signed up for the one million dollar policy you see referenced in this letter."

At this juncture, Warren paused momentarily in acknowledgement of the letter, before continuing.

"Your father opted to pay his premiums annually, but for some strange reason he always preferred to pay directly in cash and not use a check like most of my other clients. Since then, I have made it my business to stop by each year and present him with the bill in person lest it otherwise be forgotten and the policy default. And that dear sir is the reason of my visit here today."

The pointed nature of this last sentence was clearly directed at Reuven who flinched at the intended inference.

"You mean to say you expect *me* to now pay this bill?" he asked almost rhetorically.

"Well if your father is as incapacitated as you make out then *he* certainly isn't in a position to do so himself and unless there is a drastic change in his condition over the next few days he simply *won't* be able to attend to it himself."

Reuven looked again at the rather large figure being billed and then back again to Warren.

"Do I *have* to pay this bill *now*?" repeated Reuven.

Warren smiled knowingly at the question.

"You always have the option of *not* paying it and then have the policy lapse," he explained matter-of-factly, "but if your father is really as sick as you're making out that would be a rather foolish thing to do. To be more accurate, it might cost you a few thousand dollars now but you're set to get back many, many times that figure if your father doesn't make it to his seventieth birthday. To me it sounds like a wise investment decision, if you know what I mean."

Such callous indifference to a morbid prognosis for the elder Mr. Groner left Reuven quite shocked and more than a little disenchanted with the mild-mannered Mr. Maccallister. However, the strength of his argument could hardly be denied requiring more serious consideration of the offer.

"Would....would I have to give you cash right now to keep the policy active or could I send you a check later if I decide to pay then?"

Warren patiently explained that a check would be acceptable but that time was not on their side.

"To be honest, the policy officially closes in four days although the company does have an additional three day grace period after that. Any payment you'd be making would have to be received in our office by next Tuesday at the very latest otherwise the policy *would* be lost entirely."

"Okay, leave it with me until I can decide what to do," replied Reuven. "I really don't have that kind of cash available now, but maybe if my sister is willing to help we might be able to work something out."

"But of course Mr. Groner. It's your prerogative. Just don't forget that looming deadline we have to concern ourselves with," concluded Mr. Maccallister and with that final warning he bid Reuven a good evening and left the premises.

The agony of Reuven's predicament - an earnest hope in his father's survival and recovery against the actuarial prudence of investing financially in death was only compounded the next day when he met with his sister Shiri Nyack and her husband Shimon.

"NO WAY! THERE'S ABSOLUTELY NO WAY YOU CAN EXPECT US TO EVEN CONSIDER SUCH AN INANE SUGGESTION," insisted Shimon. "Some stranger shows up on your doorstep asking for *sixteen thousand dollars plus* and you even *think* of considering giving him the money and on such terms also? Reuven, I'm appalled at you! Even Dr. Dumenglume has been more optimistic for father's recovery these past few days and bringing up expensive life-insurance issues at this time is one of the most insensitive things you could have done!"

It was a fortunate thing there was soundproofing in the hospital room to muffle the noise of this vociferous outburst. In reality, Reuven had only intended to gently broach the topic at their daily meeting beside their father's bed but as soon as the subject of money had arisen his brother-in-law's wrath had been well ignited.

Ironically, Feitl's non-reaction to even these earsplitting rantings lent only further credence to Warren's recommendations and the sensibility of maintaining the life insurance.

Despite his sister and brother-in-law's staunch opposition to the project, Reuven embarked on a frantic search for funds to pay the life insurance premium anyway. The task was not an easy one and more than one potential benefactor looked askance at Reuven's stated pretext for borrowing the funds. Nonetheless his perseverance paid off and two days later he advised Warren that he had managed to amass the required sum.

"At least this way you can be comforted with whatever your father's outcome is," consoled Warren. "Obviously I wish you the best for his speedy recovery but if the end doesn't work out in his favor you can be comforted with his thoughtfulness in at least securing this policy for you these past nine years."

Reuven didn't have to wait too long to find out what that outcome would be. Several days later a significant drop in Feitl's blood pressure seemed to seal his fate and the doctors' intense efforts only succeeded in prolonging the battle a short few more days. Then, one bleak morning on the seventh of December, Feitl passed from this world, ten months shy of his seventieth birthday.

The significance of these ten months was not lost on Warren Maccallister and his life-insurance company who quickly set about fulfilling their contractual obligations under the terms of Feitl's policy. Indeed, it was Warren himself who arrived on Reuven's doorstep a fortnight later to present him with his check.

Given the sad circumstances of its issuance there was no grand presentation ceremony. There were no cameramen or newspaper reporters on hand to capture the moment for posterity. Instead Warren merely handed Reuven the sealed envelope whilst simultaneously expressing his condolences.

"Thank you for your kind and thoughtful words," replied Reuven softly as he fingered the envelope. "I guess you were right and that I do appreciate my father's thoughtfulness in arranging this check for me."

However, when the envelope was opened Reuven received a rather unpleasant surprise.

"Excuse me Warren, but I don't understand," he said to the agent. "You told me that the policy was for one million dollars, but this check is only for *half* a million. How could that be?"

"Didn't I explain that to you when we first met?" asked Warren. "Your father named yourself *and* your sister as joint beneficiaries on the policy. You've just received your check for half a million and right now I have to go over to your sister's home and present her with her check. That was after all what your father had requested."

"B…b…b…b….b…b…b…but I was the one who paid the premium though?" stammered Reuven quite helplessly. "Why should she get any of the money?"

"Well, I really don't know what to tell you Mr. Groner other than that maybe you should speak to your sister herself and try to work it out with her."

Reuven watched as Warren departed from his home then kept a firm eye on the clock, biding his time before taking action. Finally, when he was sure that Warren would have completed his second mission, Reuven firmly grasped the telephone receiver on his desk, thrust it to his ear and furiously dialed his sister's number.

Shimon Nyack picked up the phone and, much to Reuven's distaste, sounded as if he were in the most jovial of moods. In fact, he sounded happier than Reuven had ever known him to have sounded before.

"Well Reuven, I guess you were proven right after all," he said, smiling broadly down the phone. "Half a million dollars....who would have believed it?"

"Well you certainly didn't!" insisted Reuven belligerently. "Reason enough to disqualify you from receiving any monies at all from this policy payout. In fact, I insist you hand over the money to me as soon as possible to avoid any unpleasant Din Torah over the issue!"

"Any unpleasantness would be your doing, dear brother-in-law," scoffed Shimon in response. "I think the half million dollars you've already made on your morbid investment is an excellent return and can't quite see why you'd want to prolong the agony of this rather unpleasant episode any further."

☞ *Is Reuven entitled to recover all, or even part of the half million dollars Shimon and Shiri received from their father's life insurance policy? (p. 226)*

7

A Car and its Owner

It was the dreariest of afternoons. Rainclouds hung ominously low in the darkened and overcast sky and a drizzly wind was blowing from the east. But this wretched, unpleasant weather in no way dampened the spirits of the lively group of eighth grade Beis Yaacov girls as they went about their pre-Chanukah errands. First there had been the toy store in town, then a visit to Jake's Judaica, a stop at the bakery for doughnuts and finally they had to go to the bank. Bright, shiny pennies were much in demand during the *dreidle*-playing season and a steady supply for everyone to join in the fun was a necessary must.

They were not the only ones with an interest in the bank. Five minutes earlier an old and beaten 1980's Pontiac had pulled up nearby, a mysterious figure behind the steering wheel well hidden between the high coat lapels he used for warmth. As the minutes ticked by, his gaze shifted more and more rapidly between the analog, dashboard clock and the doors to the bank, as he impatiently waited for his cue.

The bank door suddenly opened and out tumbled the Beis Yaacov girls gloriously oblivious to the falling rain and the world at large in general. The old Pontiac had certainly escaped their attention, except for Shulamis Broomberg's, who had noticed it immediately upon her leaving the bank. Horrified, she watched the car leave the curb where it had been parked and drive right up to the sidewalk next to where she was standing. Panic rose in her chest as she swung around desperately, searching lest one of her friends had noticed.

But her friends had not seen, remaining entirely unaware of the car's appearance. Not wanting to lose the opportunity Shulamis made a sudden dash for the front passenger door, yanked it hurriedly open and quickly dove inside.

"Abba, what are you doing here!" she cried to her father in a whisper. "I thought you were meant to be at work now."

"Yup, I was meant to be," replied Chaim Broomberg matter-of-factly, "but Ima said you would be by the bank so I made an extra special effort to stop by and save you walking home."

"Well thanks," replied Shulamis, ducking down. "Now can we quickly get out of here please?"

"What's the matter?" asked Chaim, noisily putting the car into gear. "Didn't you want a ride home?"

"You know dad!" answered Shulamis peering through the cracked rear windshield ensuring she hadn't been seen. "It's the car! It's mortifying!! If my friends see me in it, I'll never live it down."

"Well, it's done our family very nicely for fifteen years," Chaim announced, quickly dismissing the disconcerting sentiment, "and if you ask me it's good for another fifteen too. If your friends have a problem with that then I really can't help them."

Fortunately for Shulamis the drive home went without hitch and they were soon comfortably indoors and out of the rain. However, Chaim soon discovered there were other weather-related errands to which he needed to attend.

"Feivy just called from the Browns," Shaindy Broomberg mentioned to her husband as he removed his coat, "and he needs a ride home. Would you mind so much just running out and getting him?"

Happy to oblige, Chaim was soon outside the Browns' home anticipating a grateful reaction from his soon-to-emerge son. Sadly though, Chaim's magnanimous chauffeuring gesture was not met with the level of gratitude he had expected.

"I thought Ima was going to come for me in her car," Feivy said sounding none too happy. "This car is really too embarrassing to be picked up in."

Things fared no better for Chaim when he later took the younger children to the local grocery. This time it was young Mechy who voiced a complaint about the car's broken tape deck.

"Why's everyone so uptight about our car!" cried Chaim in exasperation. "A car isn't meant to be a social statement or some sort of music box on wheels. Good reliable transportation is what counts and that's exactly what this car is!"

So carried away was Chaim with his rhetoric that he failed to notice the large garbage dumpster lying in the grocery parking lot jutting out from its place. A loud scraping noise quickly awakened Chaim to this fact and although he pulled away as soon as he could, the damage to the vehicle had already been done.

"It's really only a small scratch," he explained to Shaindy later that evening. "Hardly noticeable, especially if you're standing on the other side of the car."

"That could well be," she concurred, "but don't you think it really is time to think about getting you a newer car? We can certainly afford it and the children would be forever grateful."

As true as Shaindy's arguments rang Chaim was still reluctant to part with his old and trusted four-wheeled friend. Having been his faithful servant through many turbulent times he felt his loyalties torn by the thought of replacing the vehicle for mere want of a newer model. Ultimately though, it was the upcoming holiday of Chanukah that carried the day. Although Chaim would gladly have foregone any gift receiving during the season, he felt obliged to at least take his family's words to heart and resolved to remedy the situation of his existing car.

Selecting a replacement vehicle was a simple enough task. As far as his family was concerned anything roadworthy was an improvement on the Pontiac. More difficult though was how to dispose of the old car, as Chaim discovered during his negotiations in the local dealership.

"You mean to tell me that you *won't* accept my old car as a trade-in?" he asked Stan the car salesman in total surprise. "I'm sure you could easily find a nice new home for it and probably make a handsome profit at the same time."

"Well sir," began Stan haltingly. "Pre-owned Pontiacs aren't cars we see much of a demand for around here. I would love to be able to take it off your hands for a fair price, but I really don't think it would be doing justice to our dealership. The best I could suggest is that perhaps you should try calling these people," added Stan proffering a worn and oil-stained business card. "They are always in the market for older cars just like yours."

A quick glance at the card was more than enough to make Chaim feel queasy. Deep down he had already come to recognize where the car really belonged, but a life of denial had been infinitely more appealing.

"Actually, I don't think I could emotionally handle Charlie Murphy's junk yard just yet," he quietly informed Stan. "We've seen many happy times with the old car, and to think of it being turned into scrap metal is just........... just........... just not an option I could consider at the moment."

This hurdle notwithstanding Stan was still able to complete the sale of a newer Japanese model much to the delight of Chaim's family. The fact that Stan had to subsequently navigate his way to the Broomberg home driving the old Pontiac was a surmountable challenge, quite mild in comparison to some of the other gestures he had resorted to during a decades-long sales career.

Seeing Chaim arrive outside their home brought great joy to his family, although Shaindy's reaction was tempered somewhat when Stan came into view shortly thereafter in the old Pontiac.

"Chaim, I like your new car," she commented, "but what exactly are we expected to do with the old one? I thought you were going to use it as a trade-in?"

"Stan said that it wouldn't really fit into his showroom," Chaim explained, "so I thought we'd just hold on to it for now. I know there's really not much room in the driveway for more than two cars, but if I park it right against the wall it shouldn't really get in anyone's way, don't you think?"

Although the merits of such an argument were weak indeed Shaindy kept her thoughts to herself awaiting a more propitious time to discuss permanently disposing of the car.

Strangely enough, it was Chaim himself who finally suggested getting rid of the vehicle once and for all. It happened one casual morning when his breakfast with Shaindy was interrupted by the rattling of the front door mailbox. Chaim rose to fetch the mail, disappearing into the hallway but much to Shaindy's bewilderment he failed to return. Curiously sticking her head around the corner she spied her husband standing there, thoughtfully examining one particular letter, the rest of the mail tucked neatly under his arm.

"What's caught your interest so much?" she asked, drawing close enough to realize it was actually an invitation that he was reading. "Whose wedding are we invited to now?"

"My nephew's actually," replied Chaim handing her the card. "He's getting married next month and it's just given me a great idea."

Shaindy casually perused the rather plain invitation not noticing anything out of the ordinary.

"So what's this great idea then?" she asked, unsure of what had so captured his imagination.

"I thought we could give them the old Pontiac as a wedding gift," Chaim joyously explained. "I'm sure they'll need a car to help them get settled down and it would be just the thing."

"You'll give them your old car as a wedding present?" she asked incredulously. "You really think they'll want such a thing?"

"For sure, no question!" replied Chaim confidently. "I know my sister well enough and she'd really appreciate the gesture."

Shaindy remained rather cynical of her husband's judgment until an opportunity to verify its accuracy arose later than morning. Her sister-in-law happened to call about an entirely unrelated matter providing Shaindy the perfect opportunity to broach the subject of offloading their old car as a token for the upcoming wedding.

"Shaindy, another car would be *exactly* what we'd need," exclaimed Miriam Senderowitz excitedly upon hearing the suggestion. "In fact, we were wondering just yesterday how on earth we were going to manage getting ready for the wedding with only one car without even considering what Leib and his *kallah* would do afterwards."

"Miriam, I'm so glad to hear it," replied a relieved Shaindy. "You can have the car as soon as you'd like. In fact the sooner the better.............. that is, I mean to say you don't have to wait until the wedding to collect it!"

It was hard to say if it were the Senderowitzs or the Broombergs who were more excited about the vehicle gift although it really mattered not when a mere two days later Sender Senderowitz arrived at the Broomberg home to collect the vehicle. Through previous encounters, he was already familiar with its operation and needed neither instruction nor encouragement to get into the driver's seat and prepare for the short drive back to his home.

"Okay everyone, wave goodbye!" Chaim encouraged his family as the car drove off into the distance, "and wish it good luck in its new home."

☙ ☙ ☙

The thirty first of December was a day of little significance to Chaim Broomberg or even to Sender Senderowitz for that matter. However, for the members of The Clarkston and District Country Club it heralded one of the most eventful nights of the year. Party celebrations began shortly after nine o'clock that evening and carried on right through midnight and into the wee hours of the New Year.

Very much an active participant in these festivities was a middle-aged Martin Stubbs who was partaking of the alcoholic beverages being served with less than prudent reservation. Against the better advice of his compatriots, he determined to make his own way home, full of confidence in his pathetically impaired driving capabilities.

This confidence soon evaporated when he rounded a slow corner only to have a parked car suddenly appear in the roadway in front of him, making a collision unavoidable.

With airbags exploding all around him Mr. Stubbs escaped serious injury but the same could hardly be said for the two vehicles involved. Stubbs's new Toyota had suffered serious damage across the entire front with parts of the engine left protruding grotesquely from under the crumpled hood. The vehicle he had struck had also sustained serious damage but perhaps the worst damage done was that inflicted upon Sender Senderowitz's beauty sleep. With his bedroom window directly overlooking the accident scene it was little surprise that the loud crash of the impact more than sufficed to awaken him.

Staggering groggily to the window, Sender looked down and was aghast to see that it was none other than his newly acquired Pontiac that had borne the brunt of the impact. Wary of a direct confrontation with the aggressor he picked up the telephone and notified the police of the accident, only venturing outside after a squad car had arrived shortly afterwards.

From his perspective on the ground he saw instantly how misleading the aerial view from the window had been. Whereas from above the damage had looked minimal he could see from close up it was worse than he had first thought. The driver's door had not only been badly dented and knocked out of place but it had also been pushed up against the engine hood damaging some internal components. Worse still, further inspection revealed that neither it nor the rear passenger offside door could be opened due to the extent of the damage.

Watching him conduct this reconnaissance was police inspector Alvin Macdonald who took careful note of Sender's unusual attire – pajamas, a dressing gown, furry slippers and a pair of earmuffs. This led him to conclude that Sender was almost certainly not an active participant in the crash.

"Good morning to you sir," began the officer politely. "Did you by any chance witness this accident here?"

"Not exactly officer," replied Sender, "but I was the one who called you. This is actually my car that was hit."

The officer glanced down towards the horribly disfigured bodywork before responding.

"Well, I am sorry about the damage sir but judging from the condition of the other driver I think it's quite clear what happened. If you can just provide me with the relevant documentation I'll be happy to complete an accident report for you which should help with any insurance claim."

Sender presented the registration and insurance cards Chaim had given him, silently hoping that they were in order lest he be victim of an unwanted and expensive penalty. He waited with bated breath as the officer seemed to take an unusually long time inspecting the papers. Finally he was ready to acknowledge their validity.

"Very good sir," confirmed Macdonald. "All correct and up to date. Now, is this your current address here?" he continued. "I don't recognize it as being in our immediate vicinity."

"No it isn't actually officer," replied Sender. "It's actually my brother-in-law's name and address here. This used to be his car up until a few days ago when he gave it to me."

While this explanation may have sounded plausible enough it failed to satisfy the officer who continued with an interrogatory barrage of awkward questioning.

"So it is your car then?" asked the officer.

"Yes sir."

"But it's registered in someone else's name."

"Errrrr, yes sir," replied Sender more nervously. "Is that a problem?"

"Problem? I'll say! It's totally illegal! You can't own a car and then have it registered in someone else's name! That's fraud that is."

Fortunately the officer was in a genial mood and was able to offer an equitable solution to the problem.

"Now let me ask you this," he began, "Are you sure you haven't just *borrowed* this car for a couple of days instead?" he asked suggestively. "If you have then I can just write a report with this fellow's information down and we'll be done. That'll be so much easier than having the vehicle towed and impounded, wouldn't you agree?"

"Of course officer whatever you say," confirmed Sender. "That's exactly how it is. I've just borrowed it for a couple of days."

This seemed to placate Macdonald enough for Sender to leave the scene and he quickly ventured back indoors and out of the cold. Officer Macdonald likewise retreated to the warmth of his squad car to complete his report, the sleeping figure of Martin Stubbs securely seated in the car's rear.

Twenty minutes later the officer was back at Sender's door proffering a copy of the accident report.

"All the information you require is here," explained Macdonald showing him how the report had been laid out. "Just call this fellow's insurance company at the number given here and they should set you straight. If you have any further questions you can always call me down at the station," and with that Officer Macdonald bade him good night and a happy new year.

Following the officer's advice Sender filed a claim with the drunken offender's insurance company and found them very courteous and accommodating. They helped him file the claim, apologized profusely for their client's behavior and promised to deal with the matter in a prompt and efficient manner.

ଔ ଔ ଔ

It was breakfast time at the Broombergs once again. Chaim and Shaindy were enjoying a few relaxing moments together when the familiar rattling of the mailbox broke the silence. As had become their custom, Chaim rose to fetch the mail while Shaindy waited vainly for his return.

"Chaim, is everything okay out there?" she called into the hallway. "What did you find today in the mail?"

"Shaindy, you won't believe this but we just received a check for fourteen hundred and twenty two dollars from some insurance company in Seattle."

"In *Seattle*?" questioned Shaindy. "Are you sure?"

"Yes," confirmed Chaim. "The Seattle Car and Home Insurance Company sent us the check on behalf of their client, a Mr. Martin Stubbs. It says that this is in full settlement of our claim against him for the damage done to our old Pontiac."

"For the Pontiac?" repeated Shaindy. "I thought Sender had junked it. What's this money about?"

"Well he only junked it because it had gotten smashed up," explained Chaim, "but I had no idea there was any insurance claim involved."

"But why fourteen hundred dollars though," continued Shaindy. "The car was in such a state it couldn't have been worth anywhere near that figure."

"I don't really know," replied Chaim. "I guess that must be the way the company calculates the loss based on their estimate of the vehicle's worth. Still, I'm certainly not complaining about it."

"Well," smiled Shaindy. "I guess you were right all along and it was a good idea to keep the old car. I'll call Miriam up right now with the good news. With the wedding this week I'm sure she'll be especially grateful for the extra money."

Chaim looked puzzled.

"Why are you calling her up?" he asked worriedly. "What's this got to do with her?"

"Well I thought that really the check should go to them, don't you think so?"

"You mean to say that you intend giving this entire fourteen hundred dollars to her?" Chaim exclaimed, sounding rather horrified. "Why would you want to do that? We already gave them the car and if they went ahead and got it smashed up that's their problem. But this check is *ours*," he concluded, gleeful dollar signs flashing in his eyes.

"But Chaim, the insurance money is for the car and since it was their car that got smashed then they should get the money?"

"No they shouldn't," he said firmly. "I would never have given them fourteen hundred dollars for a wedding present and if the insurance company sent *me* the check, then it's because they want *me* to have the money!"

☞ *Who does the insurance money really belong to?* *(p. 228)*

8

Tutor Trouble

With feelings of dread, Aharon and Nechie Neumann attended the parent-teacher conference in their daughter's school. From the beginning of that year eight-year-old Dina had been struggling to keep up with the class and despite encouraging parental incentives her marks had still been sadly lacking. While the teacher had tried to be understanding of her failing pupil, the need to keep up with a rigid curriculum allowed for little latitude in the classroom. The Neumann's had been kept aware of this deteriorating situation by the brief, curt notes that regularly appeared on Dina's homework sheets pointing out sharply the need for improvement.

Unfortunately, the more the year progressed, the more impatient the teacher appeared to become. It was against this harsh backdrop that Dina's parents attended their first joint face-to-face meeting with Mrs. Natanchik. Predictably, after exchanging pleasantries, the teacher gave her brutal synopsis.

"We've tried everything to help give young Dina a boost this year but as I'm sure you've noticed it's been without success. I really feel at this stage it would be appropriate to hire a tutor to assist Dina with her schoolwork. Having her continue to struggle at this point would be a shame when simple intervention would surely solve the problem."

Aharon would have liked to launch into an accusatory monologue about the possible poor atmosphere or lack of positive reinforcement in the classroom but Nechie prevented him, aware of the futility of such an exercise.

"This is just something we'll have to sweat out for the rest of the year," she said to him resignedly, "and anyway, maybe Dina really could use the extra help and attention."

ଓ ଓ ଓ

The quest for a suitable tutor started that very same night. The obvious choice had been the previous year's teacher but maternity leave quickly nixed that idea. Another suggestion had been Nechie's high-school aged niece but the pressures of upcoming examinations and a taxing social schedule assured she too was unavailable. Other more professional tutors also expressed little interest in the project; being the middle of the school year most were either already fully booked or unwilling to take on the strict regimen for which Mrs. Natanchik was calling. Eventually though, Nechie's persistence bore fruit when a friendly neighbor approached with a possible suggestion.

"My niece just got married and moved to town less than a month ago," explained Mrs. Brown, "and I know she's been looking for a job. Maybe this would be just the thing to interest her?"

A skeptical Nechie's initial reaction to the idea was somewhat negatively tinged.

"Does she know anything about teaching third grade studies?" she asked guardedly. "We can't just hire anyone for Dina. It has to be the right person."

"Well I know she did some teacher training in seminary and she is just the nicest, kindest, friendliest person you could ever hope to meet," replied Mrs. Brown reassuringly. "I'm sure Dina would do wonderfully with her."

Despite Nechie's reservations over the idea, a lack of any other immediate alternative prompted her to follow up her neighbor's recommendation with a phone call.

As it was, Mrs. Brown's information proved to be quite accurate. From Ashira Reich's telephone manner it sounded as if she was indeed as kind-hearted and caring as one could have hoped. However, as Nechie had intuitively pointed out, Ashira herself had some reservations over accepting the appointed task.

"I don't know what to tell you," she said hesitantly upon hearing Nechie's predicament. "I hadn't really thought much about tutoring. I was looking more for a full time job. But tell me anyway, what exactly are you looking for?"

Patiently, Nechie described the details of Dina's curriculum and her present standing in the class.

"She really is a bright girl, but is just having trouble with this particular teacher," Nechie finally said. "I'm sure you'll find her to be a very bright and receptive young student."

Ashira hesitated before finally giving some sort of acquiescence.

"Okay, I guess it does sound like a worthwhile project. Let's schedule an initial lesson so I can get to meet Dina and we'll take it from there. How does tomorrow sound?"

"Tomorrow after school would be perfect," confirmed Nechie. "Where do you live?"

"I'm at twenty six Orchard Grove, in the new apartment building."

"In Orchard Grove?" asked Nechie quickly, quite taken aback. "You mean in that tall, modern, gray building?" - the Orchard Grove residences were very exclusive and not a place Nechie was in the habit of frequenting.

"Yes, exactly," confirmed Ashira. "To get to our apartment you'll take the elevator to the fourth floor and we're at the end of the corridor on the right."

"Good!" confirmed Nechie "I guess we'll both see you then tomorrow, shortly after four."

ও ও ও

The following afternoon saw mother and daughter finding their way into the Orchard Grove Condominium. Soon the plush elevator was whisking them up to the fourth floor from where they followed the opulent corridor to its end. Reassuringly, Ashira was there waiting to greet them.

As she had sounded on the telephone, Ashira's manner was bright and forthcoming, considerably helping to put Dina at ease. The pretty dinette table offered ample space to lay down her schoolbag and a waiting glass of orange juice was just the tonic to help Dina acclimate further. All seemed ready but Nechie had one or two issues left to clarify.

"How long do you think today's lesson will take?" she asked Ashira politely. "I hope it won't be too long for a first time."

Ashira looked towards Dina who looked quite comfortable and at home before replying.

"Probably about three quarters of an hour. If you come back at five o'clock we should be done by then."

"And we didn't manage to finalize a price yet either," continued Nechie in a more muted tone. "How much will you be charging us?"

Ashira was equally uncomfortable at broaching the subject of money, neither wanting to sound mercenary nor overly forgiving.

"I….I don't really know," she stammered nervously. "I hadn't really given it much thought. I suppose I'll just charge you whatever the going rate is. It shouldn't be hard to ask around and find out."

"Oh, that's fine then," confirmed Nechie; she had been secretly concerned Ashira would quote an elevated figure reflective of her affluent lifestyle something not at all consonant with the Neumann budget. "So I'll see you at five o'clock then."

ଔ ଔ ଔ

As could have been predicted Dina responded well to her new tutor and was in excellent spirits when her mother arrived at the end of the session.

"I think it's worked out very well today, don't you think so Dina?" Ashira asked, turning to her budding pupil. "Shall we schedule again for tomorrow at the same time then?"

Dina looked happy at this prospect, sufficient reason for Nechie to agree.

"And it's fine if you just pay me at the end of the week," added Ashira amiably.

The days passed quickly with Dina faithfully attending her lessons with a final session on Friday afternoon. When Nechie arrived to collect Dina, Ashira gave her a most glowing report of their progress.

"I must say we had an excellent week together didn't we Dina," she said warmly. "We covered most of her math and English and she'll be ready for her *Chumash* test on Monday if she'll just spend a few minutes reviewing over *Shabbos*."

"That's wonderful!" exclaimed a grateful Nechie. "I'm glad you were able to accomplish so much with her in such a short space of time. Now how much is it then that I owe you?" she asked, removing a checkbook from her handbag.

"Well let's see then," began Ashira. "Dina was here four times this week and at sixty dollars a lesson that works out to be two hundred and forty dollars in total."

"How.....how much did you say that was per lesson?" said Nechie trying not to sound too shocked.

"Sixty dollars. I asked a few of my friends and that seems to be the going rate."

"Okay," replied Nechie quite taken aback at what sounded like an astronomical figure. "I guess that it's two hundred and forty dollars then."

The check was soon written out and received gratefully by Ashira who seemed eager to repeat their schedule the following week.

"That should work out," replied Nechie haltingly, "but let's wait until after Shabbos before scheduling anything. I'm not sure what's on this coming week and just need to check a few things first."

What she had really meant to say was check that she had not been horrendously overcharged, for Nechie had never imagined tutoring could be so costly. However, Ashira's obvious naïveté combined with Dina's innocent listening ear sufficed to prevent Nechie from being so uncouth and instead she politely exited the apartment with Dina, wishing Ashira a friendly, parting Good Shabbos.

Almost immediately upon their arrival home Nechie took to the telephone to try and clarify if Ashira's rates were indeed in line with reality. Her first call to one of the tutors she had contacted the previous week yielded surprising results.

"The average tutor charges about thirty to thirty five dollars a lesson," she was told. "You might find it cheaper if you shop around but thirty is generally regarded as a fair price."

"Thirty?!!" exclaimed Nechie. "Are you sure? I just got charged two hundred and forty dollars for only four lessons which works out to be more than *sixty* dollars an hour."

"Sixty? That does sound expensive. You might find that very experienced teachers or educational specialists can get away with charging that much, but from my experience the price should be considerably less. Unless of course the lady you went to is like a proper professional."

"No, not at all," said Nechie numbly, and anxiously called the next number on her list to check the matter again.

"I actually like to charge forty dollars per lesson," said Mrs. Braithwaite, "but if I feel that's too much of a burden to the parents I'd probably drop it to thirty five and keep the lesson down to slightly less than an hour. But sixty dollars does seem like a lot to me. I mean you can always find people in demand that charge whatever they want, but I don't see most tutors getting away with it."

While Nechie was fairly fuming after these two calls, her husband encouraged her to remain calm and call a third tutor to confirm what seemed to be an emerging picture.

"Sixty dollars a lesson? That's real, professional, top-of-the-line rates," was Mrs. Davidson's response to the question. "I charge thirty five a lesson which I think is a fair price. If I'd charge much more I'd probably lose most of my clients."

Infuriated, Nechie called Ashira shortly before Shabbos, struggling as best as she could to suppress the growing anger exploding in her chest.

"Hello Ashira," Nechie began, not waiting for a response. "Before confirming lessons for next week there is a small matter I'd like to clarify. We agreed that I would pay you the going rate which seems to be around thirty dollars a lesson. I thought you were supposed to be proficient in mathematics so how you arrived at a figure of two hundred and forty dollars for a mere four sessions is beyond me. According to my calculations we actually overpaid you one hundred and twenty dollars but it's fine if you apply that extra money as credit to the lessons this coming week. Dina would actually like to come this Sunday, Tuesday, Wednesday and Friday if that would work for you."

Ashira however was as taken aback as Nechie had been.

"The days that you mentioned would be fine for tutoring Dina, but I'm not sure what you mean by any credit." she explained. "I hope you don't think that I just made up a figure of sixty dollars a lesson and then charged you that without doing my research. I actually asked quite a few of my friends and they all told me that sixty dollars a lesson is a fair rate. Maybe there are some people who charge less but in all probability they're only worth that. I mean, you have seen for yourself how happy Dina has been here which is all part of the service."

Despite the eloquence inherent in Ashira's every word Nechie remained quite unmoved.

"That was a lovely speech, but quite frankly, Aharon and I aren't at all interested in spending that kind of money. We think the correct thing would be for you to charge rates more in line with normalcy instead of listening to your fancy friends and their big ideas."

"Oh dear, I beg your pardon! I am sorry," replied a startled Ashira, "This is not at all what I had expected and I really don't think it's appropriate for you to talk of my friends in such manner. I'm sorry you feel you were overcharged, but sixty dollars is the rate and is not negotiable."

☞ *Is Ashira entitled to charge the full sixty dollars for her services as her investigation suggested is the going rate?* *(p. 231)*

9

Destination Beijing

The first thing Jeremy felt was the heat. It hit him immediately upon leaving the airplane, a hot portent of what he had to expect during this first visit to Beijing. Sweating profusely, he battled the humidity through passport control and baggage reclaim before exiting through customs. Pausing briefly to inhale, he took stock of his situation, gazing down at the mesmerizing, churning sea of perspiring humanity that crowded the arrivals area. In every which direction people were rushing, some laden with heavy baggage, others struggling to keep up with their companions. And it was in this madness and confusion that Jeremy was expected to find and locate his waiting taxi driver!

Certainly there was no shortage of drivers and chauffeurs. Literally hundreds of them jostled en masse for position on an endless line, each holding signs that to Jeremy all looked Chinese. After futilely studying the line for some tense moments he was startled to hear an unfamiliar voice emanate from out of the crowd calling his name.

"Mista Berga! Mista Berga! Ova hee pleeze Mista Berga!"

Unsure the voice was addressing him personally Jeremy looked into the crowd and saw a small oriental figure waving at him furiously.

"Mista Berga! Mista Berga! Hello and welcome to Beijing," said Huey Chango. "Allow me to take you'h bags and I'll show you the way to the ca'h."

Dumbly, Jeremy followed the strange figure glad at least to be getting away from the deafening racket of the arrivals hall. The driver also seemed happy to let the surrounding noise fade into the background allowing for conversation in a more normal tone.

"Mista Berga, I hope you had a nice flight. My ca'h is just over he'e, and you'h hotel is quite close by."

"I'm really glad to hear it," yawned Jeremy. "There's nothing I need more now than a nice comfortable bed."

"You no sleep on the plane Mista Berga?"

"Errrrrrrrr…., no actually. Why do you ask?"

"This must be you'h fi'hst time in China, right Mista Berga?

"Why y…y….yes! It is actually," confirmed Jeremy quite taken aback at his driver's seemingly psychical powers of deduction. "How do you know that? And how did you know I was Mr. Berger to start with anyhow?"

"You were the only person wea'hing a hat! And my people with hats from America always fly business class after thei'h fi'hst time of not sleeping in economy."

"You know," thought Jeremy. "That sounds like a most comfortable idea," and he quietly dozed off in the back of the taxi.

That the journey had tired him so seemed to have little bearing on Jeremy's business prowess. He spent that entire week going from one successful meeting to another his person apparently having found favor in the oriental eye. Even Huey Chango seemed sad to see Jeremy leave, almost shedding a Mandarin tear as he dropped Jeremy back at the airport for his return flight.

"Goodbye Mista Berga" he said emotionally, "and I 'ope you come back again soon."

"Okay, goodbye Huey and thanks for all your help."

ଋ ଋ ଋ

It was some twenty hours later that Jeremy arrived back home much to the delight of Mrs. Michal Berger and the rest of the family. However, while *she* eagerly wanted to hear news of his far-east adventures, *he* desperately craved the restful recluse of a warm bed.

"What are you so tired from?" asked Michal. "I was hoping you'd have had ample opportunity to rest up on the way home."

"Are you kidding?" he yawned back. "The plane ride was impossible. I would love to have slept but it was just impossible. The guy on my right next to the window fell asleep straight away and snored loudly for most of the way. I would have tried leaning more to the left, but this tall husky basketball player type firmly placed his hand on the armrest even before take-off and that's where it lay the entire flight. After sitting sandwiched like that for fifteen hours I'd be *bentching gommel* even if we hadn't flown anywhere!"

"Oh dear! How terrible for you!" sympathized Michal. "I had no idea you'd come back such a *shmatte*."

"I had no idea either," agreed Jeremy. "In fact, if old Saffer asks me again I'll have to tell him that this long haul flying is just not for me!"

"Good idea! You tell him just that," agreed Michal wholeheartedly.

However, conveying this powerful message to Morris Saffer, Jeremy's munificent employer was not such a simple task as Jeremy discovered two months later. Then, as before, he found himself standing in front of his boss in the intimidating surroundings of the overly plush sumptuously furnished office.

"We just got a call from Mr. Chen Chawong," began the company chief executive officer in a deep commanding voice. "He was one of our contacts you met in Beijing and he stressed that we need to send someone out to meet with one of our main suppliers there. We feel that for the good of the company you would be just the man for the job. Do you think you'd be able to do that for us?"

This was a mission Jeremy did not at all relish, the discomforts of the previous trip still fresh in his mind.

"How long would I need to be away for sir?" asked Jeremy not knowing how else to react. "And when would I need to go?"

"At the beginning of next week and for about four days in total. Is that okay?"

"It should be fine," replied Jeremy knowing that it wouldn't. "But let me first clear it with my wife at home and see if it's okay with her."

While this maneuver did give Jeremy temporary relief, it didn't exactly solve the pressing nature of his situation. Indeed while Michal was certainly devoted to her husband's job, four days absence at short notice with the prospect of an exhausted returning-home spouse was not something she lightly dismissed. Nonetheless, ever loyal to his company position Jeremy attempted to paint for Michal a most convincing argument, placing himself as the epicenter of another mega-global vital entrepreneurial scheme.

"He really needs you *that* badly?" she asked skeptically.

"Well, yes," confirmed Jeremy. "He said that the man in China even asked for me by name which doesn't often happen with these big companies."

"I don't know what to say," Michal mused. "You came back such a wreck last time, I really don't know if it's worth your while to keep on doing this."

"So I should just tell him 'no' and finished?" offered Jeremy sounding rather downbeat. "He won't be very happy about that."

"Well maybe I have a better idea for you then," suggested Michal thoughtfully. "Why not tell Saffer that if he really needs you to go to China that badly he should fly you there First Class! That way I'm sure you'll manage to get plenty of sleep en route."

Whilst this sounded like a fair compromise it did leave Jeremy with the delicate burden of shuttle diplomacy that would make the Chinese meetings seem simple in comparison.

"WHAT DO YOU MEAN YOUR WIFE SAYS YOU NEED TO FLY BUSINESS CLASS?!" Morris Saffer asked Jeremy heatedly upon hearing the request. "Do you have any idea how much that will cost the company? Those fares to the far-east are very expensive especially this time of year."

"I know sir but my wife does have a point considering how tired and exhausted I was after the last trip," Jeremy offered back weakly

"Why do you have to mix your wife into this anyway?" continued Mr. Saffer. "Why not just tell her that you're going and finished!"

Before Jeremy had an opportunity to formulate a response, their conversation was interrupted by the secretary's voice sounding over the intercom on Morris's desk.

"There's a call for you sir on line one."

"I'm in a meeting now. It'll have to wait."

"But it's your wife sir, and she said it was important."

Mr. Saffer growled inwardly, exchanging a knowing look with Jeremy before picking up the phone to take the call.

"Yes dear, what it is?...... Yes I know......Yes Greta I know...... I told him this morning......Yes I know...... No, that was after the garbage......Yes of course dear......I'll do it on my way home...... pink...... Yes I know......Yes dear......

Okay I really must go now...... yes okay goodbye dear, goodbye."

With a sigh of relief Morris was finally able to end the call and turn his attentions back to his meeting with Jeremy.

"Now where were we then?" he asked.

"We were discussing my wife's request that I fly first-class to China next week sir," replied Jeremy *extremely* flatly.

"Mmmmmmmmm...... Your wife's request you say...... Oh well cogito ergo sum I suppose. She does have a point. Okay I'll approve it this time. I'll authorize an extra fifteen thousand dollars for your expense account which should cover the cost, and...... errrrr...... Berger, just remember," continued the CEO in a calm, commanding voice that conveyed ultimate authority, "anything you may have overheard in this office is of course highly confidential, you do understand that don't you?"

"Oh sir, yes of course," beamed back Jeremy. "Confidentiality is my middle name, sir."

"Well, just make sure it remains that way young man. Now off you go and start preparing for your trip."

☙ ☙ ☙

It was a triumphant Jeremy who arrived home later that day to share the news with his family. While Michal was not particularly thrilled at her husband's forthcoming absence she nonetheless had to acknowledge that Mr. Saffer's first-class gesture was an indication of just how vital her husband was to the enterprise, quieting any remaining objections she still harbored.

Aside from his wife, Jeremy was equally eager to share the details of his upcoming trip with others too.

"That's first class, I'll be traveling," he proudly announced to his friends after *shul* that evening. "Not something that happens every day."

"That's really swell," replied Heshy Kahn duly impressed.

"Very nice for you," added Duvy Green.

However, it was Ari Kaplan, the travel agent who was the most excited with this news.

"First class to Beijing?" he said interestedly. "No problem Jeremy. Just call me in the office tomorrow and we'll take good care of you."

Jeremy followed Ari's lead that very next morning and called the agent with all his travel details.

"I need to arrive in Beijing before Tuesday morning and be back here for Shabbos. Do you think you can manage that?"

"Sure, sure," replied Ari the travel agent. "Just hold on and let me check for you right now."

Jeremy listened to the sounds of Ari's hurried strokes on his computer keyboard before the agent's voice was heard again, detailing the results of his flight search.

"Alright, if you want we can have you coming out of Kennedy on Sunday afternoon which will have you touch down in Beijing well in time for a Tuesday nine a.m. meeting. Return is Thursday morning and you're back home Thursday night, easy. Total price in business first is fourteen thousand three hundred and twenty two dollars and sixty seven cents plus a twenty dollar booking fee."

"Sounds okay? Who's that with?

"Air China."

"Mmmmm. Anything similar with a US based carrier maybe?" asked Jeremy cautiously.

"Okay let me check for you and see what comes up."

Jeremy waited for another few seconds, while Ari's keyboard continued its furious drumming.

"I have something similar out of La Guardia at four o'clock Sunday if you'd like. That's with……with………... one second," Ari began mumbling half to himself. "That's with Quebec Air?"

"Quebec Air?" repeated Jeremy. "Who are they?"

"That's what I'm wondering," replied Ari as he continued typing. "They're actually a small Canadian airline and I don't see how they could be flying from New York to China," he added sounding quite puzzled. "Give me just one second here……………………now I've got it!" he called out triumphantly. "It's just a code-share flight with American Planes International."

"Oh good!" said Jeremy with relief. "American Planes are a great airline. How much is the fare with them?"

"Let me just check for you……………... That'll be fourteen thousand four hundred and eight dollars including all taxes. That's only marginally more than Air China's fare. Would you like me to book it for you?"

Jeremy hesitated slightly before replying.

"I suppose that if you could match it to the Air China price then I'm sure it would be fine. I don't want to overspend my budget unnecessarily."

"Fine okay, leave it with me," said Ari, "and I'll get back to you later on this afternoon."

Jeremy spent the remainder of the day attending to his routine affairs, the airline business of his morning all but forgotten. Consequently, when Ari's call eventually came in Jeremy was merely expecting confirmation of their previously discussed arrangements and not prepared for the agent's obvious eagerness to discuss anything else.

"Jeremy, are you sitting down?' asked Ari his voice brimming with excitement.

"Yes, I guess I am," replied Jeremy hesitantly. "Why? What's up?"

"How would you feel about departing from Mirabel International rather from JFK?"

"Mirabel?" Asked Jeremy slightly surprised. "Isn't that near Montreal? Why would I want to fly from there? Didn't you say you could get me on a direct flight from New York?"

"Sure I could, if you wanted me too," explained Ari, "but considering that the fare from Mirabel is around *four thousand dollars* cheaper than from New York, you might just want to consider it."

"FOUR THOUSAND DOLLARS," Jeremy heard himself echoing. "Wow that is a lot of money! Are you sure? Maybe there's a catch or something."

"There is, but tell me if this isn't funny. The reason it's cheaper is because it's not a direct non-stop flight. It actually involves a two-hour stopover in...wait for it.... *New York* of all places."

"You mean to say that...."

"Precisely! Quebec Air's flight leaves from Mirabel and then connects with the American Planes' direct flight from New York. If you pick up the plane in Montreal then you'll certainly save yourself a nice tidy sum. And if you only have hand luggage I can even fly you back into New York without you having to take the connection back to Montreal."

Jeremy was excited at the thought of these savings but the logistics were still lacking.

"That all sounds very nice," he said, "but how exactly am I meant to get to Montreal in the first place to catch the flight back to New York?"

"That's easy," replied Ari confidently. "I could easily get you a ticket for around one hundred and fifty or so. You'd have to leave on the eleven fifteen to make the connecting one fifty five flight back to New York but apart from a few hours extra travel on the outbound I think you're basically set. Sounds good, no?"

"I guess it does," agreed Jeremy. "Okay, go ahead and set it up for me for next Sunday."

As instructed, Ari made the necessary reservations, sending Jeremy a confirmatory e-mail when he had completed the job. Jeremy received it the next morning, gratefully noting that Ari had not forgotten to book him kosher meals. However, he found the attached receipt and itinerary rather cryptic and confusing.

Ari Kaplan Travel Agency

RECEIPT FOR ITINERARY AS SHOWN

New-York - Beijing - New York

PAID IN FULL

Dep. 17th May 2007

Ret 21st May 2007

Passenger .....Mr. Jeremy Berger

One business class ticket... $14,422.22

Fortunately one quick call to Ari's agency cleared up the confusion.

"You should just ignore what it says on the receipt," explained Ari reassuringly. "You're flying through Montreal as shown on the airline schedule and you've been charged precisely ten thousand four hundred and ninety four dollars and change for both tickets in total. The receipt you're looking at is the one you submit to your company accountant for reimbursement. It'll be their job to ensure that your expense account authorized the ticket and the price is correct, which it is."

"You mean, I bill the company for the New York ticket and then only pay you for the Montreal ticket," he asked. "Are you sure that's okay? I mean it does sound a bit dishonest doesn't it?"

"Not at all," said Ari reassuringly. "After all, you are going through the extra bother of flying out of Montreal which your boss had no intention of making you do. As far as he's concerned the money on the ticket is already as good as spent, so what difference should it make to him if you profit instead of the airline? Believe me Jeremy, this is very much standard business practice and you needn't bother thinking about it again."

☞ *Is Jeremy allowed to submit the false invoice and claim his full allowance for the trip?* *(p. 232)*

10

The Rosh Yeshiva's Matzos

It was Adar already yet it seemed as if the semester had just begun. Heshy, Duvy and Leiby had spent close to a year learning in a Jerusalem yeshiva, maturing into serious and diligent students. Many factors had combined to assure this end. An appropriate apartment with friendly yet sincere *bochurim* had provided a solid base and the yeshiva environment itself had been highly conducive to spiritual advancement. Even their stomachs had acclimatized to the harsh yeshiva food, negating the need for nocturnal pizzeria visits, and freeing the time for extra study. This assiduousness was patently evident in their everyday conversation.

"Hey Leiby! Whattcha doin' Purim?" asked his friend Nachman Hyams.

"*Tosfos* on *daf Tess*," came the prompt reply. "The Rosh Yeshiva said we'd need to know it for *shiur*."

"How about you Duvy?" continued Nachman, in search of a more recreational response. "Going anywhere interesting?"

"You bet!" came the excited reply. "Heshy and me made up to speak to the Rosh Yeshiva about that *sugya* he spoke out in the *chabura* last week. Normally he's too busy to give us extra time but because some of the *bochurim* are away he was able to fit us into his schedule. Maybe you'd want to come too?" he offered. "It's really an opportunity you wouldn't want to miss, right?"

The trio's diligence continued unabated through the next few weeks and it took the inquisitive questioning of Nachman to remind them of the fast approach of the end of the semester.

"Say Heshy, when are you leaving for the *zman*?" he asked curiously. "I heard there's a lot of trouble with flights this year and if you haven't booked yet you might just end up staying here for *Pesach*."

"I don't know," replied Heshy. "I hadn't really thought about it much. I guess I'll probably go back just after *Rosh Chodesh*."

Nachman approached Duvy and Leiby with the same question but found them equally detached from serious consideration of their flight options home.

"I did hear a couple of the guys saying flights were hard to get," mentioned Duvy, "but I didn't pay much attention. Still, if you also say there's a bit of a crunch on seats then maybe we should start thinking about reserving."

The next afternoon Heshy contacted a local travel agent who confirmed the rumor Nachman had been circulating.

"I'm afraid your friend is quite right," explained Mrs. Braham, "and the flights are extremely busy this year. But

I'll see what I can do anyhow. When would you like to fly and how many people are you?"

"There's three of us and I suppose we should try and fly out as soon as possible after *Rosh Chodesh*," reasoned Heshy. "What do you have available?"

Mrs. Braham worked furiously trying to accommodate the threesome but found it a harder task than she had envisaged.

"Getting the three of you off together is difficult," she finally said. "However, I do have two seats available on the third and the ninth is also open if you'd like, although with *Yom Tov* beginning on the eleventh that doesn't leave much time for delay."

Heshy's noble character promptly dictated how to proceed with this information.

"Okay then, you'd better book my two friends Duvy and Leiby on the flight on the third," he allowed. "I'll risk flying on the later date."

"That's very selfless of you," replied the agent. "I hope it works out okay."

"I'm sure it'll be fine," replied Heshy dismissively. "In any case, I have an uncle here who I could always stay with if I get stuck."

Although the third of April was well in advance of *Pesach* it was almost a week *after* the official end of the yeshiva semester. Nonetheless the Rosh Yeshiva was more than happy to accommodate his students' extra diligence.

"In fact I'm sure it's *min hashomayim* that the flights were full," he remarked to them. "You never know, maybe there's a good reason that you got delayed these extra days," he added with a twinkle in his eye before leaving the room.

"Duvy, what on earth was all that about?" Heshy asked as soon as the Rosh Yeshiva was out of earshot. "What's he hinting at? He never wastes his words for nothing!"

"I don't know," replied Duvy. "But Yehuda will probably know what's up. Let's finish up working on today's *chazora* and then we can go back to the *dira* and ask him."

Back at their apartment, Yehuda seemed impressed at their intuition.

"You're right!" he confirmed. "The Rosh Yeshiva *was* hinting at something. Every year around this time he bakes his matzos together with a very select group of *bochurim*. He's very meticulous and employs a lot of stringencies during the process so he only takes *bochurim* who really know what's going on. But this year some of last year's group left and now he's on the lookout for new helpers to train in. I'm sure he must have his eye on you if that's what he said."

"Baking matzos with the Rosh Yeshiva!" exclaimed Heshy in awe-struck joy. "That sounds fantastic!"

"Yes," confirmed Yehuda. "It is a good opportunity and you can even get to buy some of the matzos at the same time. People from everywhere are after them but they're just not for sale to the general public."

"You know, those matzos would be just the thing for my father," commented Duvy thoughtfully. "I was looking for a present for him and they would be exactly what he'd want."

"Mine too," added Leiby. "He's always on the lookout for new *chumros* and matzos from the Rosh Yeshiva...... that would be just amazing."

"Yes they would make an excellent gift to the right person," confirmed Yehuda, "but that's only if things works out in time. The bakery isn't known as the most reliable in its timekeeping and they might still push us off until after you've left."

Naturally this highly confidential subject of the matzo baking was soon the talk of the entire remaining yeshiva body, keeping the *Beis Hamedrash* abuzz with excitement during those few post-semester days.

"When did they say the baking would take place?"

"I thought it was meant to be at the end of this week."

"Someone said tomorrow."

"But that was yesterday."

"Now it changed until after Shabbos."

"I heard they got held up by a big *chabura* from Tel Aviv and now they're talking about the week before Pesach."

Avidly following these developments were Heshy, Duvy and Leiby with Duvy and Leiby especially concerned.

"Yehuda, when *exactly* do you think they'll be baking?" pressed Duvy again for the umpteenth time. "My flight's on the third and it'll be such a letdown if we don't bake before then."

"Your guess is as good as mine at this point," Yehuda shrugged. "The bakery gave some excuse about one of the workers being off sick which got them behind schedule on their main orders so they've pushed us back again I'm afraid. It's going to happen eventually like every year, although when is anyone's guess."

It was a nail biting next few days for Duvy and Leiby as they followed the ever-changing saga of the matzos. A fixed date of the first had to be revised at the last moment to the third because of a delay with the flour and then, as that deadline approached another delay occurred because of a supposed power outage. Eventually with the hours remaining before their flight home rapidly diminishing Duvy and Leiby finally had to resign themselves to the reality that they would not get to bake with the Rosh Yeshiva and instead have to return home to regular matzos.

With these sobering thoughts running through his mind, Duvy had a sudden flash of inspiration and he quickly rushed over to the *Beis Hamedrash* in search of his friend.

"Listen Heshy," said Duvy calling his old *chavrusah's* attention. "The Rosh Yeshiva's going to bake any day and I've just got to get hold of a box of those matzos for my father. Maybe you could do me a favor and bring a box with you when you come?" he asked. "Here's fifty dollars which should more than cover the cost and we can worry about the change a different time."

Heshy hesitated before taking the money, a smile spreading across his face.

"I was actually waiting for you to come and ask me," he said pulling an identical bill from his pocket. "I already got this from Leiby who was here just before and asked me the same thing! Like I said to him; they're meant to bake tomorrow and unless there's a major delay it shouldn't be a problem."

Much to Heshy's delight, the baking did indeed take place that very next day and it was an experience he would long treasure. The work started long before the appearance of any ingredients, as the Rosh Yeshiva showed the group how to inspect all the bowls and surfaces for the minutest trace of remnants from previous doughs. Then, with the mixing of the flour and water the action really began.

"QUICK! HURRY! DON'T STOP! *L'SHEIM MATZOS MITZVAH!*" cried the Rosh Yeshiva continuously as he circled the work floor again and again, ensuring the workers wouldn't slack nor leave the dough stagnant for even a moment. Heshy worked hard at rolling his dough, then watched in awe as his cry of *'MATZO'* saw his kneaded circle whisked away for combing and baking, all within a matter of seconds.

The group's efforts continued in such vein for slightly more than two hours after which time they had to stop and make way for another *chabura* that had scheduled to bake.

Heshy followed his fellow workers into the packaging room where the fruits of their labor were amply evident. Boxes full of matzos were piled high to the ceiling and two other huge trays holding scores of other matzos stood nearby waiting to be packaged.

However, as plentiful as this supply seemed, it was still not enough. After each worker had received his quota there only remained a few boxes and although Heshy had merited a well-earned box of his own, procuring matzos for his friends was a far from simple task.

"But I also need to buy a box each for Duvy and Leiby," he tried explaining to the Rosh Yeshiva's *gabbai*, holding out the two fifty dollar bills he had received as if to reinforce his claim. "It's not their fault that the baking was delayed until after their flight home yesterday."

"I'm sorry, but we're shorter than we imagined," explained the *gabbai*. "Not all of the matzos were baked crisp enough and the Rosh Yeshiva had to reject them. We still had a few pounds left over but Moshe Mandlestam, one of the Rosh Yeshiva's big supporters is coming for *Yom Tov* and we felt obligated to provide a few boxes for him and his family."

Dejected at the failure of his mission, Heshy turned to leave the bakery protectively clasping his single box of the precious matzos.

"Heshy! Come back quickly" he heard the *gabbai* suddenly calling. "We found some more matzos for you!"

Heshy rushed back, almost bumping into the Rosh Yeshiva who was on his way out laden down with his own matzos.

"Heshy, *l'at, l'at*," said the Rosh Yeshiva in a calming, fatherly voice. ""We've finished baking now, at least for this year anyway."

Aghast at the near disaster that had almost befallen him, Heshy corrected his step and made his way back to the *gabbai* in the packaging area.

"I managed to get you one more box," he told Heshy. "I know you wanted more but at least this is something."

Gratefully Heshy paid and took the matzos back to his apartment pondering all the while how he would bring them home intact. Finally he resolved to transport them in his hand baggage, an idea which met with favorable results as a sympathetic member of his flight's cabin crew helpfully placed the boxes into a first-class overhead bin. Assured of their safety Heshy sat back and relaxed in his economy seat for the flight home.

ೞ ೞ ೞ

New York:

Two days before Pesach, 5768

"Ma, could you use any help? There must be something I can do for *Yom Tov*."

Henny Grossman looked lovingly at her son, aware his offer of assistance was coming merely hours after his nearly day-long journey home.

"Heshy, that is so kind of you! I'm really managing just fine here. Maybe you should try and get some rest instead after your flight."

"No it's really okay, ma," he replied. "If there's nothing for me to do then I think I'll stop by the *Beis Hamedrash* for a couple of hours until *Mincha*. After that, maybe I'll lie down for a bit."

As Heshy prepared to leave, Mrs. Grossman looked on with silent pride at how much her son had benefited from his year away.

Almost equally excited at Heshy's reappearance in New York were his friend's Duvy and Leiby who also happened to have been in the *Beis Hamedrash* that day.

"*Sholom Aleichem*," Duvy said, greeting him warmly. "We were a bit nervous you wouldn't make it in time for *Yom Tov*."

"It really wasn't such a big deal after all," Heshy replied casually. "I knew I'd get back in time."

"So you've brought the matzos then?" asked Leiby quickly. "We're relying on them for the *seder* at home."

"Us too," added Duvy. "Can I get them from you after *Mincha*? I told my father and he was really excited."

"Well, actually there was a bit of a problem," Heshy slowly explained, "and I was actually only able to get hold of *one* other box."

"Only *one* other?" repeated Duvy, slowly digesting the stress's inference. "I presume that must have been for me then, right?" he added hopefully. "After all, we were *chavrusos* together last zman."

"What do you mean?" countered Leiby. "I gave Heshy the money before you did so I get it first isn't that right Heshy?"

Heshy looked first at Duvy, then at Leiby and then back at Duvy again. They both seemed to have valid reasons predicating they should be the one to receive the precious matzos.

"I don't know what to tell you," he finally said, "but I've an idea. When I get home after Mincha I'll call the Rosh Yeshiva then and I'll let him decide for us."

Duvy and Leiby both agreed this sounded like a fair and equitable solution and the three promptly turned their attentions back to the far more pressing issue of a difficult *Tosfos*.

ꙮ ꙮ ꙮ

"Hallo, Kopplestein here." The Rosh Yeshiva was invariably brief and succinct, not wasting words even when it came to answering his home telephone.

"Yes, th…th…this is Heshy Grossman speaking, from America."

"Heshy! *Mein teireh talmid! Vos macht ihr*? How can I help you?"

"Well actually we needed to ask the Rosh Yeshiva's advice in a difficult matter," began Heshy and continued to relate the entire dilemma of what to do with matzos. In typical style, the Rosh Yeshiva deferred his decision to a much more conclusive authority

"You don't need me to help you decide this question," he told Heshy. "This very case has already been *paskened* for you in *Shulchan Aruch!* Go and look it up for yourself!" and he proceeded to give Heshy the exact reference, before ending the call.

☞ *What is the Halacha the Rosh Yeshiva was referring to?* *(p. 233)*

11

Catered Caper

The office was small and unprofessional but Yoel and Chana Safir were glad to be there anyway. They were seated opposite Ovadia Cohen of Cohen's catering and the topic of discussion was the upcoming Bar *Mitzvah* of their son, Gedalyah.

"Now maybe we can decide on which kugels you'd like to choose," asked Ovadia trying to finalize the details of the event. "Our standard *Kiddush* package gives you a choice of regular potato, lokshen, sweet yerushalmi, salt and pepper yerushalmi, apple, broccoli and of course, the all time favorite, overnight potato. Do you have any preferences?"

This wonderful choice was more than enough to fire Yoel's imagination and with his salivatory glands on high alert he asked for a simple favor.

"I'm not quite sure," he replied. "Can we get to sample them first to help us decide?"

This atypical request did catch Ovadia off guard momentarily but fortunately Chana stepped in to diffuse the moment.

"No, I really don't think that'll be necessary," she interjected. "I think we already decided on the sweet yerushalmi and the overnight potato. Now, how about salads? Something bright and colorful would be nice to tone in with our cream and gold color scheme. What would you suggest?"

"Wait a second," interrupted Yoel. "We didn't finish with the hot menu yet. Is *cholent* included in the base price or will it be an extra?"

"Of course it's included," Ovadia assured him warmly. "How could one enjoy a *Kiddush* without a generous helping of my best *cholent* and with *kishke* too? Au contraire my friend, hot *cholent* is *the* hallmark of a Cohen *Kiddush*."

"Good, I was worried about that," confirmed Yoel.

"Are you sure we want *cholent*?" asked Chana with some reservation. "Remember that fiasco last month in *shul* when someone's *cholent* burned and the smell came in through the air conditioning and disturbed everyone. Maybe it would be safer not to have a *cholent* just in case?"

"Mrs. Safir, you needn't worry," said Ovadia reassuringly. "I have specially designed pots with accompanying hotplates to keep the *cholent* just the correct temperature to simmer overnight without risk of getting too dry. Burnt *cholent* is really something I'm not familiar with. The only complaints I get are from the Rabbis who say the tantalizing aroma of *cholent* wafting through the *shul* distracts people's attention from their *droshos*!" he laughed.

"Now, let's get back to the salads again. What was it you were looking for again?"

Their conversation continued in similar vein for another half hour until all the details of the entire Shabbos had been clarified.

"So it's all finalized then," said Ovadia beginning his summation. "For the Friday night meal we'll be catering for fifty people with the menu I've just printed up for you. My waiters will set everything up and serve and all you'll need to do is just relax, sit back and enjoy your guests' compliments. Afterwards, I'll have my staff clear everything away and make sure they're back on Shabbos morning well before your eleven o'clock estimate of when the *Kiddush* will begin. That way they'll be ready to serve without delay as soon as the *davening* has finished."

"Wonderful!" said Chana gratefully. "I feel relieved already, knowing it's in your hands."

This comment carried more weight than the caterer could have realized. The previous month Chana's sister had also made a Bar *Mitzvah*, but had tried to economize and cater the event herself.

Unfortunately, it had not gone as smoothly as had been hoped, a shortage of disposable cups being only one of the more notable miscalculations that had marred the *simcha*. Being busy with many guests arriving from abroad and their concurrent accommodation requirements, Yoel and Chana reasoned that petty paper ware worries were just not something they wanted to be busy with during their *bchor's* Bar *Mitzvah*. Ovadia Cohen's all-inclusive package seemed to be just the right solution.

They weren't the only ones seeking out Ovadia's services that Shabbos. Rabbi Shaya Shendro and his family were celebrating the *aufruf* of their son and the rabbi's prominence in the community almost certainly assured a large turnout at the *Kiddush*. As it was, Ovadia Cohen had a long time affiliation with the great rabbi and it was only natural that he be in charge of the event, his previous commitment to the Safirs notwithstanding.

Ordinarily, even catering two separate events in different locations at the same time was well within the capabilities of the caterer. He had ample staff, efficient, well-trained managers and generally enough equipment to keep everything running smoothly. However, that particular week a shortage of one item threatened to impact negatively on the quality of his service. Given the lateness of the hour, and with time pressures building, he unprofessionally turned to his client for assistance.

"Mr. Safir, hello this is Ovadia here. ……..No don't worry, everything is fully under control and we're ready for your *simcha*. There is perhaps just one small thing you could maybe help with. I was wondering if you would have a hotplate we could use for the soup tonight. It's not too urgent but I would very much appreciate it."

Always eager to help others Yoel was unhappy to have to deny the request.

"I'm sorry Mr. Cohen but we really just don't have one."

This negative response succeeded in extracting only the quietest of sighs from the caterer, but Yoel had heard it and was quick to come up with an alternative solution.

"But don't worry though," he quickly continued. "It just so happens I have to stop in at the *gemach* shortly for something for the house and I can ask them for a hotplate as well. I'm sure they'll have a spare one and if not we'll still manage fine with the soup. Please, don't worry yourself unnecessarily about it."

An obviously rather busy Ovadia was delighted to hear this solution not doubting for a moment the *gemach* would come through and his soup would be the correct temperature.

"Fine, wonderful, good," he said quickly. "Just bring it to the hall sometime before Shabbos and we'll set it up for you along with everything else. Goodbye!"

As Yoel had predicted the *gemach* did indeed have a spare hotplate and obligingly lent it to him. Placing it in the rear of his car together with various other Shabbos requisites Yoel brought it to the hall later on that afternoon but to his surprise Ovadia and his crew were nowhere in sight. With only one hour remaining until Shabbos, Yoel was left imagining a worst case scenario wherein he would have to cater the whole thing himself and worse still, have to break the news to Chana! Fortunately he did not have to agonize for too long for moments later the screeching of a hastily driven truck heralded the arrival of Ovadia and his crew in all their glory.

"Ah! Mr. Safir perfect timing I see," remarked Ovadia upon greeting his client. "We were slightly delayed at my last stop, but we've still got plenty of time to set you up and get ready for tonight's meal." With this reassurance given, Ovadia began issuing rapid instructions to his men who immediately got to work emptying all they needed from the truck.

An amazed Yoel stood back in wonderment as they brought out *challahs,* cakes, cookies, fish platters, meat platters, fruits, vegetables, pickles, olives, salads, mayonnaise, *chrayne* and crate after crate of sodas, waters, fruits and grape juices. These were soon followed by heavy boxes of crockery and flatware, tablecloths, linens, serving dishes and utensils, hotplates and a large quantity of disposable plastic cups, plates, forks, knives, spoons, serviettes and even cute little shot glasses. Last, but certainly not least was all the hot food. More than impressed already, Yoel watched in mouth-watering awe as huge pans of *kugel* were followed by trays of chicken, meat, potatoes, vegetables, soup pots and the largest *cholent* pot he had ever seen.

"As you can see we plan everything down to the last detail," Ovadia commented, noticing Yoel's fascination with the preparations. "My men are well trained and will have everything set up for you in no time at all. Now did you bring the hotplate I mentioned earlier? I'll need it now for the soup to make sure it stays properly hot for the meal tonight. Some caterers just boil the pot up before Shabbos and hope it stays warm, but we like to do things properly."

Yoel amiably pointed out where he had left the hotplate and, satisfied all was in safe hands, left for home to assist Chana with the children.

ᘓ ᘓ ᘓ

It wasn't until two hours into Shabbos that the Safirs and all their guests were finally assembled and ready to begin the *seuda*. With quiet satisfaction, Yoel swept his eyes approvingly across the crowd seated at the exquisitely laid tables, secretly amazed at how quickly Ovadia's men had affected the turnaround from a hall of chaos to one of orderly elegance.

At Chana's gentle prodding he began leading his family and guests with a traditional rendition of *Sholom Aleichem* followed by a soul-stirring *Eishes Chayil*. The Bar Mitzvah boy himself made *Kiddush* and soon all had washed and begun the meal.

"I say, this whitefish is good isn't it Chana," remarked Mr. Owitz to his daughter. "And the pickles are really crunchy too."

Yoel smiled in response.

"Ovadia's only been in the business for a few months but he did come highly recommended and now you know why. They say his food's the best in town!"

As if to add compliment to these musings, Ovadia's waiters were soon on hand to quickly and discreetly remove the fish plates, clearing the tables in advance of serving the soup. Knowing how well hot chicken consommé chases whisky, Yoel brought on to the table an admirable selection of Scotch and liqueurs, offering generous glassfuls to all who wished to partake.

It was a fortunate thing for Yoel to be on the better side of a good dose of alcohol when the next course was being served. In fact, he hardly noticed what was amiss altogether until Chana discreetly shared a private word with him.

"Yoel, what happened with that hot plate you brought for Ovadia?" she asked worriedly. "I thought you said he was using it for the soup."

Yoel, now aware that his plate of steaming chicken broth was actually far from being close to steaming, could only shrug his shoulders in quiet resignation.

"It's still passable so let's just hope the guests don't notice," he whispered back. "Frankly, I'm more worried about my speech than anything else."

Yoel's great speech notwithstanding, by the time main course was served it was patently obvious that something was going seriously wrong in the kitchen. Not retaining heat as well as soup, the solid foods served next were very definitely much below acceptable serving temperature.

Although the guests seemed content to nibble and chew on cold pieces of chicken, Chana and Yoel were becoming increasingly upset at the developing failures of the evening meal. Excusing himself politely, Yoel ventured behind the scenes and into the kitchen where he found the waiters quietly apologetic over the lack of heat but entirely helpless to do anything about it.

"You do realize this is a terrible embarrassment for me and equally unpleasant for my guests," he told them sternly.

"Very sorry sir," they said helplessly, "but the hotplates not working properly and everything cold."

Seeing the futility in continuing the conversation Yoel resigned himself to let the waiters continue serving the ice cream when, just as he was leaving the kitchen the large pot of *cholent* in the corner caught his eye. Transfixed, his entire body seemed to take on a mind of its own as his limbs propelled him over to the corner as if on automation.

He stopped barely twelve inches from the pot and, in a move of agonizing foreboding, stretched out his hand to touch its side. The nerve endings on his outstretched fingertips instantly conveyed the dreadful news to his fuddled brain; STONE COLD. The *cholent* pot was STONE COLD! Close to fainting, he walked over to where the trays of *kugel* were stacked and found them equally poorly heated.

"All hotplates not working," the headwaiter superfluously informed him. "This never happened before."

"Well, what do we do now?" Yoel asked near panic. "We have over two hundred guests coming for *Kiddush* tomorrow and there's NO WAY I can serve them cold food."

"Don't worry sir," answered the waiter. "I'll go speak to Mr. Cohen after the meal and he'll know what to do. You can just go back and sit down for the ice cream."

Yoel emerged ashen-faced from the kitchen and was instantly greeted by Chana who had guessed from his dull pallor what he had discovered.

"The *cholent*'s also cold, right?" she asked knowingly.

"Yes," he confirmed, "and the kugels and EVERYTHING. When I get hold of that Ovadia I don't know what I'll do to him."

"Listen, I'm sure it's all *bashert,*" she said comfortingly. "There's still plenty of food for everyone and they'll just have to manage without *cholent*. And if they don't like it, too bad for them!"

"Yes, I suppose you're right," he replied still unbelievingly. "*Ah bi milept*!"

"Now let's get back to our guests and forget about it until later, okay."

This sagacious advice could not be argued with, especially given the public setting, and Yoel soon reclaimed his place at the head table for the meal's conclusion.

☙ ☙ ☙

Whether or not the waiter ended up speaking to Ovadia later that evening was of little relevance since there was nothing to be done anyhow. The food would be cold and that was it. Fortunately though, as Chana had predicted, there was still plenty to eat for everyone and Yoel even tolerated one or two complimentary remarks about the benefits of a simpler *Kiddush*. It wasn't until the evening though, after Shabbos had gone out, that a full post-mortem on the day's events took place.

The culprit of the day was soon discovered. A flipped breaker in the hall's electrical panel was ample testament to what had gone wrong.

"How could you have overloaded the circuits with all those hotplates?" cried Yoel accusatorily to Ovadia. "Anyone could have told you it would blow the electric."

"Not at all," challenged the caterer. "I've been in this hall many times with even more heaters and nothing like this has ever happened. There must have been another reason for the electricity to blow like that."

To discover the real source of the problem, Ovadia began to reconstruct the events of the previous day. He flipped back the breaker, plugged in all the hotplates and watched as within five minutes the breaker flipped off again.

"That just shouldn't be happening," he said again, quite mystified and even more determined to get to the root of the problem. One by one he removed the hotplates from the wall sockets, and watched in wonderment as the breaker still continued to flip.

Finally, realization dawned upon him and, as simple experimentation soon proved, it was the *gemach* hotplate that was faulty and had repeatedly short-circuited the electricity each time it was connected.

"Well at least now we know what went wrong," he sighed, casting an accusatory glance in Yoel's direction. "I knew it couldn't have been anything to do with me or my equipment."

"That may well be," commented Yoel, "but it doesn't change the fact that our Shabbos was ruined and there's no way I'm going to pay you for all that wasted cold food."

"What do you mean?" pressed Ovadia quite firmly. "We just proved that the whole fiasco was your fault because of your hotplate. I did everything I was meant to and you messed it all up. It's bad enough that my reputation has been so tarnished but for you to threaten not to pay is just beyond comprehension."

"Well," replied Yoel with considerable self-control. "Rather than senselessly argue about it, why don't we go and ask someone who knows what the correct thing to do is and let them decide."

☞ *Does Yoel have to pay for the cold catering? (p. 234)*

12

Salary for a Son-in-law

Ethel Harrisman was an expert at homework. Having been a junior school teacher for many years she knew exactly how to carry out the various tasks, papers and projects that were part and parcel of every child's nightly routine. However, her sterling expertise was put sorely to the test one evening as she examined her eight-year-old son's prescribed assignment.

"Yossi, what is this *mishnayos* work you've been given?" she asked puzzledly, trying to decipher the Rebbi's scrawl. "Are you meant to be *teitching* it or what? And where can we find a *mishnayos* at home?"

Unfortunately, looking towards her son for guidance was a futile exercise. Yossi had only just begun *mishnayos* in school, leaving him only slightly less mystified about the work than his mother.

"I think we're meant to say it over with the *pshat* also," he finally answered.

"And can you do that by yourself?" asked Ethel hopefully.

Yossi paused momentarily before replying.

"I'm not sure Mommy," he said. "Maybe."

Try as he might though Yossi couldn't quite figure out precisely what *Halacha* the *mishna* was saying or how the different concepts fitted in. After twenty minutes of fruitless struggle Ethel was finally ready to give up.

"Okay Yossi, I think that's enough homework for tonight," she said in resignation. "We're just going to have to leave the rest to your father."

Although this solution may have sounded quite logical, implementing it was a most difficult task. Josh Harrisman ran a very tight schedule, not arriving home until past eight o'clock on most evenings leaving precious little time to devote to third grade homework studies.

"I'd love to learn with Yossi more," he explained to his wife later that evening, "but you know how crazy my timetable is. Between *Maariv, Daf Yomi,* the gym, the *Halacha* shiur and the basketball league there really isn't time to sit down with Yossi to do nightly homework."

"But what's Yossi meant to do then?" pleaded Ethel. "You can't really expect me learn *mishanyos* with him. It's just beyond my scope."

"Don't be so negative!" said Josh impatiently. "I'm sure the Rebbi knows just how busy fathers are these days and would almost expect the mothers to do the homework. Just go through the sheets Yossi brings home and I'm sure he'll do just fine."

Alas, this optimism was sadly misplaced as Josh, and more importantly his father-in-law, discovered a few weeks later during the upcoming *Yom Tov* of Succos………..

ଔ ଔ ଔ

"Come over here Yossi!" called Mordy Rothman from the comfort of his leather armchair. "Come and tell me what you've been learning in school."

Yossi slowly extricated himself from the engaging board game taking place on the floor and made his way over to where his grandfather was seated.

"We just starting learning *mishnayos* this year," he answered proudly, feeling particularly grown up and only slightly aware of his own incompetence.

"Wonderful!" said Mordy. "Tell me, what *mesechta* are you learning?"

"*Mishnayos Brochos*," answered Yossi quickly.

"Really!" replied his grandfather. "When I was a young boy we also learned *Mishnayos Brochos.* Maybe we could learn some together just now?"

Yossi confirmed his interest in the idea and together, grandfather and grandson retreated to the quiet refuge of the study. Mordy pulled a *sefer* from the bookcase behind him and was soon seated at his desk next to the young Yossi.

"Okay, here we are then," he said placing the volume down before them. "Let's hear what you've learned this year so far."

Yossi found the correct page, put his finger on the place and began with gusto.

> *"mei......mei....... mosai koreen es sh'ma beerveen, meesha shehikonim neeeeeechnoseen le'echol beeeeeetroo....beetromosson."*

It took Mordy every effort not to wince from pain at his grandson's woefully inadequate rendition. Instead he feigned unawareness over the poor performance as Yossi struggled along until *Mishna Alef* had been completed.

"Very nice, very nice indeed," said Mordy trying to sound proud. "You did very well especially as you've only just started *mishnayos*. When I was much younger," he continued, drawing Yossi closer, "we had a *mishnayos* Rebbi with the biggest moustache you could ever imagine. One day..........," and he continued relating some small anecdotes bolstering his grandson's spirits after the slightly demeaning *mishnayos* experience. Half an hour of quality time later the two returned to the rest of the family happy and laughing, with Mordy quietly determined to improve his eldest grandson's *mishnayos* endeavors.

Naturally he felt his son-in-law was to blame. Yossi was a smart boy and there seemed no reason for his failing other than a lack of concerted parental effort and assistance.

Now, although confronting one's son-in-law is neither simple nor opportune, Mordy sought out an opening nonetheless. That opportunity came during a pleasant family walk home from *shul* on *Simchas Torah* night. After crossing the main town thoroughfare together, Yossi and his younger brother ran ahead giving Mordy Josh's undivided attention.

"I see Yossi has already begun *mishnayos*," began Mordy pleasantly. "This certainly must be a milestone for you, having a son up to that stage already."

"Yes, it is," agreed Josh. "It seems like only yesterday that we were celebrating his *Bris*, and here we are almost nine years later and he's learning *mishnayos*."

They walked on together for another few paces before Mordy made his next move.

"Do you ever get a chance to learn with him yourself?" he asked feigning ignorance. "I'm sure it must be difficult with your tight schedule."

"Well it is quite difficult actually," sighed Josh resignedly, "but we do spend some time at the Shabbos table going over what the kids learned during the week. In fact, some of the *Divrei Torah* Yossi says over are quite advanced for his age."

"At the *Shabbos* table?" cried Mordy sounding quite appalled. "That's not good enough for a boy of Yossi's age! You really have to make it your business to take the time and *chazer* over his *mishnayos* with him on a regular basis. You must have realized that he isn't exactly as fluent in them as a boy with his capabilities should be."

Josh attempted to minimize any urgency in the situation but his father-in-law's determination was to prevail.

"Listen, I know it's hard for you, but this has to be something you take seriously. Relying on Ethel to do *Chumash* and *kriah* is fine, but *mishnayos* is entirely different and having her try figure out what to do just isn't going to work."

"I guess you do have a point," acknowledged Josh with difficulty. "I suppose I should take out the time to sit down with him more often."

Sensing victory at hand, Mordy now played his trump card.

"I'll tell you what," he began in a thoughtful tone. "I'll give you one hundred dollars a week if you make it your business to sit down and learn with Yossi without any distractions for two hours during the week. What do you say to that? Is that fair? Do we have a deal?"

This offer more than startled Josh and he didn't quite know how to respond.

"Are you sure?" he finally asked. "I mean it's only a few *mishnayos* we're talking about and I'm sure it could be done in much less time than that. And don't you think two hours a week is a bit much for such a young boy?"

"That's exactly my point!" replied Mordy quite forcefully. "People today are so quick to brush aside what should be a priority in life. It wasn't like this when I was a young boy. Our parents weren't running all over the place and they made sure to give each child plenty of attention and quality time. I wouldn't have gotten to where I am today without having been treated as a human being when I was younger and you should try and be there the same way for your kids."

Sensibly, Josh realized how important this issue really was to his father-in-law and made no further excuses.

"Okay, I'll give it a try," he said, mentally searching for a slot in his schedule to fit in those hours. "I guess Yossi really could use the extra time."

ꙮ ꙮ ꙮ

Over the next few weeks, Josh discovered that learning with Yossi was more of a pleasure than the imposition he had originally feared. An *avos ubonim* program in their local *shul* afforded an excellent opportunity to learn for an hour each *motzei Shabbos* and splitting the second hour into three or four shorter sessions easily fulfilled his father-in-law's prescription.

Ethel was equally enthused by her husband's interest in the project but perhaps more than anyone else it was Yossi who benefited from the arrangement. His improving proficiency was soon noticed both by his fellow students and his Rebbi, further helping him mature into a fine mishnayos student indeed.

Against this backdrop Chanukah arrived and the Harrisman family were back again visiting their Rothman grandparents.

"So Yossi, how have you been keeping?" asked Grandpa Mordy, taking note of his grandson's relaxed poise and confident air. "You look like you've had a good last couple of months."

"Oh yes, *Zeide*!" he replied eagerly. "I even moved to the top of the class in my school and my Rebbi is so proud."

"Really?" chortled Mordy, quite pleasantly surprised. "I'd like to hear this for myself."

Beckoning Yossi to join him in the study, Mordy took the appropriate volume from its place in the bookcase and placed it down on the desk as an invitation to his grandson to begin. Yossi confidently sat down, found the place and, with his young face a mask of adult concentration, began his rendition in a clear and determined voice.

> *"Mei'eimosai koreen es shema b'arvin, from when do we begin lehning the shema in the evenings,"* he chanted. *"Meesha shehakohanim neechnoseen le'echol betroomosson, from the time when the kohanim come in to eat their Teruma. Explains the Bartenura, any of the kohanim who had become Tomei beforehand toiveled in a mikvah during the day and were then allowed to eat terumah after nightfall. From this we learn that.........."*

Mordy continued listening with wonderment as his grandson completed a flawless recitation. The contrast with the dismal performance a mere eight weeks earlier was readily apparent and even Reva, Mordy's wife noticed the difference.

"Wasn't it nice how well Yossi said his *mishnayos* today?" she commented to her husband. "He seemed to really know them."

Also eager to discuss his *b'chor*'s learning achievements was Josh. While certainly he derived a good deal of pleasure at his son's achievements, Josh was equally eager to collect on his father-in-law's remunerative pledge. The money earned since Succos had already been well spent and Josh was fairly relying on receiving his eight hundred dollar check before the evening was over.

However, despite Josh dropping numerous delicate hints, his father-in-law seemed entirely oblivious of their previous arrangement. Left with little other choice Josh poised himself to gently but firmly confront his father-in-law over the forgotten wages.

"I guess fathers-in-law can also be right sometimes," he began nervously. "Yossi really has made tremendous progress, and all because of the couple of hours a week we've been spending together," he chuckled.

"Yes it was a good idea, wasn't it," responded Mordy more as a statement of fact than as a question. "It's always a good thing when parents spend time with their children and Yossi's progress is ample proof of that."

"Ahem, yesssssssss," hummed Josh politely agreeing. "But didn't you also mention something about money for learning with Yossi? I was hoping you would make good on your promise and pay me for the eight weeks of learning we did so far. At one hundred dollars a week, that's now eight hundred dollars."

"I should pay you for learning with your own son?!" Mordy snorted derisively. "You must be joking! You should have been learning with him yourself even before I intervened! Just be happy with the lesson I've taught you about what a wise investment of your time it is to learn with your son. Forget about any money!"

Josh was shocked.

"But you did mention that you would pay though, didn't you? Doesn't keeping your word mean anything to you at all?" he said quietly.

"Sorry, did you say something?" asked Mordy in flat denial. "I didn't quite hear you clearly. Was it something important? Maybe I need to get my hearing tested?"

But Josh had by now understood he would not better his father-in-law in this instance and reluctantly let the matter rest.

☞ *Is Mordy allowed to withhold the money he committed to pay his son-in-law for learning with Yossi? (p. 236)*

13

Cheesecake

From its humble exterior, the petite coffee shop looked like any other. Plaid curtains framed the old showcase that stood just inside the window and an ancient, weather-beaten sign hung unassumingly above the doorway stating simply, "Pastries and Bakeshop".

Yet within these hallowed walls labored Pierre Waldenbaum, a genius of the culinary trade. Day and night he toiled, creating the most delectable of fruitful pastries, savory delights and petit foures. Indeed, the smooth textures and melodious flavors infused into his every gourmet creation were only matched by the beauty and elegance of his exquisite presentations. From far and near many would come to sample his work, leaving perhaps a tad heavier at the waist and significantly happier at the palate.

It was into this tantalizing boutique of the edible kind that Tzvi Rothbaum had occasion to enter one bright summer afternoon.

"Ah Tzvi, my good friend, how are you today?" boomed out an exuberant Pierre. "How good it is to see you again!"

"Oh thank you Pierre, it's good to see you too," said Tzvi as the wonderfully sweet aromas of fresh baking reached his nostrils. "How are things doing? It smells like business must be good."

"It is," confirmed Pierre, "and all thanks to *you* my dear friend. I can never forget how good and kind you were to me when I first opened the store. While others were predicting how quickly I would close, you gave me the confidence and courage to continue; to bake, improve, experiment and perfect. And now, look! Pierre's cheesecake is famous all over the world. Without you Tzvi, I might well have given up and then what? No cheesecakes, perish the thought!"

"Oh, please Pierre, it was nothing really," said Tzvi bashfully. "Just a matter of recognizing real talent when I saw it."

"Tzvi my friend, you are too kind. But please, don't let me waste time chattering endlessly. Do tell me, how I can be of assistance this fine afternoon?"

"Well, to tell you the truth I actually came in for some cheesecake."

"Cheesecake, for you? Certainly! Please, let me serve you a slice on the house. Which flavor would you like? I would recommend the blueberry today. The fruits are so fresh and bursting with flavor it really is magnificent."

"That's very kind of you Pierre. I'm sure they are. No today I need one cheesecake, chocolate flavored and also..."

"You want to buy a *whole cake* today Tzvi?" interrupted Pierre. "I'm so flattered! Are you having a party or something else I should know about?"

Tzvi chuckled warmly.

"No! I mean, not me anyhow. It's actually my brother-in-law from the city. He called me this morning with a most unusual dilemma….."

ଔ ଔ ଔ

"Tzvi, how are you? Mona here. What's doing?"

"Fine, great. How about you?"

"Good! Are you coming into the city for Uncle Chaim's Bar *Mitzvah* tonight by any chance?"

"Yes, we were actually planning on it. Why do you ask?"

"It's just that I need to ask you the biggest favor, but this is strictly confidential until tonight, okay? Our Malki's been meeting this boy for around two weeks and would you believe it they're already about to get engaged. Sylvia and I never dreamed this would happen so quickly and we're really unprepared to make a *vort* or a *l'chaim* or anything at all. Ordinarily we'd have just served up some franks and things but being the nine days that's out. Really we'd prefer to wait until next week to announce the *simcha* but the *shadchan* won't let us wait that long so it'll probably happen tonight instead."

"Wonderful!" congratulated Tzvi. "So what can I do to help?"

"Well you know that guy near you who makes those great cheesecakes?"

"Sure! You must mean Pierre from the patisserie."

"Exactly! He's the guy. Anyhow, Sylvia thought it would be a good idea to serve up a few of his cakes as centerpieces- maybe three or so, and work around them with the rest of the set-up. Would you be able to pick them up and bring them with you?"

"I guess we could manage," confirmed Tzvi. "But are you sure you want *three*? They're not small cakes you know and not cheap either."

"Three would be perfect and money's no object! Just make sure they're well wrapped and don't get ruined on the way....."

ଋ ଋ ଋ

"And so Pierre, here I am needing not just one but *three* whole cakes."

Pierre's ebullience at his friend's celebration knew no bounds and he leapt around the counter to plant a kiss firmly on Tzvi's cheek.

"That is so nice for your cousin. Hopefully by your children also! Now, let me see," he said thoughtfully. "A chocolate cheesecake I have in the back already boxed and packaged so that's a good start. And there's a delightful marble-crumble cake coming out from the oven in about three minutes, so that will be two. Now, what can I do for you for a third one...."muttered Pierre as he pondered the matter. Finally his eyes fell upon the still intact strawberry and kiwi cake that lay atop a patterned pedestal platter protected by an ornamentally-shaped clear Lucite cover. Pausing only for a moment, he reached inside the showcase, removed the entire platter and placed it on top of the counter.

"And here we have number three," he proudly announced. "Let me just get the other two for you and then you can be on your way."

Pierre retreated to the back of the store and returned carrying two large sturdy boxes which he placed next to the strawberry-kiwi cake that still lay inside the pedestal platter. Jotting briefly on the notepad that lay near the cash register he totaled up the bill and presented it to Tzvi.

"Tzvi my friend, your total bill today is one hundred and twenty dollars. Is that not a good price for you?"

"One hundred and twenty?" exclaimed Tzvi. "That can't be! That's far too little! It can't be more than a half of what you would normally charge."

"But of course dear Tzvi," said Pierre warmly. "For a friend like you this is the least I can do."

"But I already told you it's not for me," objected Tzvi. "It's for my brother-in-law and he'd be more than happy to pay you full price. Here, let me give you the full two hundred and forty right now."

"No I cannot," maintained Pierre.

"But Pierre, you must!" insisted Tzvi again. However, no amount of cajoling or argument could convince Pierre to accept more than his originally stated price and Tzvi, against his better nature had no choice but to acquiesce to Pierre's generous demands.

"Please, let me help you to your car," continued Pierre. "These cakes are quite heavy."

"That's really not necessary. Why don't you instead box this fruity cake while I take out these other two and that'll save us both time," suggested Tzvi.

"No, I want you to take the cake and the platter as they are now," replied Pierre. "Why should I waste time boxing a beautiful presentation like that?"

"But it's your platter though," cried Tzvi fearing another unwelcome contributory gesture from this amorous benefactor.

"I know but the design is really quite out of date and I've been meaning to get rid of it anyhow and modernize the showcase. Really, you'll be doing me the biggest favor by taking it off my hands. Please, I'm sure you could make good use of it in the future."

This plea from the heart more than convinced Tzvi of Pierre's sincerity and he begrudgingly agreed to take the platter as was. Together, the two carried the cakes out to Tzvi's car ensuring they were safely secured in the rear seat, after which Pierre bade his friend a very fond farewell.

Tzvi's final port of call before leaving for the city was home to collect Zlatte, his wife. All ready for the trip, she opened the car door to find a place for her wig stand only to discover the boxes and platter occupying the entire rear seat. The fruitful cake upon the fanciful platter in particular caught her eye.

"Tzvi, what's this fancy thing here?" she asked. "You mentioned you were bringing cheesecakes for this *l'chaim* but I can't believe Mona would have splurged on such a piece? Are you sure that's what he wanted you to get for him?"

"Actually no," said Tzvi, and went on to describe in vivid detail the entire drama that had transpired with Pierre at the patisserie. As amused as Zlatte was by his colorful tale, she was not so taken with her husband's final comments on the matter.

"One second," she corrected him. "It's all very nice that Pierre was so generous but that's only because he's got this thing about how you helped him out years ago and is no reason why Mona shouldn't have to pay full price! You just tell him straight that it was eighty dollars a cake and don't say another word!"

"Well, I don't know.... I mean that.... maybe perhaps..."

"And I hope you're not also thinking of letting *them* keep that platter either," Zlatte interrupted him. "You know how long I've wanted to get hold of something just like it and we'll just bring it back home with us after the party's over, okay?"

☞ *Zlatte insists that her husband is the rightful benefactor of Pierre's generosity, both with the platter and the price discount. Is she correct?* *(p. 238)*

14

Suit Sale Saga

It was a joy filled summer for the Manies family. Twenty five year old Batya had recently become engaged and preparing for the September wedding was a most enjoyable way to spend the summer. Fischel Klapman too had his own reasons to be thankful for the timing of his sister-in-law's upcoming wedding.

"I *am* glad your parents chose to make Batya's *chassuna* at the end of the summer," he remarked to his wife Fayge as they walked towards the town shopping precinct. "Imagine having to buy a new suit at full price! At least this way we get to take advantage of Mendy's great summer sales."

"Really Fischel, I'm surprised at you!" replied Fayge sharply. "My parents have waited long enough to see Batya getting married and the least you can do is happily buy a suit for the occasion without compulsively obsessing yourself about the cost."

"I was just trying to look on the bright side you know," he replied as some sort of justification.

"Well, you'd better get used to bright sides," replied Fayge as they continued walking. "Hopefully Yocheved will get engaged soon now that Batya's off the market and when she does you'll be getting a new suit for her wedding also, whatever the price."

"Maybe not," replied Fischel excitedly as they came upon the large sign hanging in Mendy's Suit Store window. "It looks like Mendy's are having another one of their famous 'two for the price of one' sales again. I can buy two suits now and just keep the second one for Chevi's wedding whenever that well be."

While conceding to her husband on his suit logic, Fayge had more pressing concerns when it came to the subject of dealing with her spinster sister.

"Rather than worry about your clothing it might help if you'd do a bit more to try and find her someone to marry. There just don't seem to be any nice boys out there for her."

Fischel shrugged his shoulders in brief acknowledgement of his sister-in-law's plight, turning instead to the more immediate task of perusing the store's wares.

Finding the section of suits sized thirty-six medium was not a problem and soon Fischel was fully engrossed in the task of finding something appropriate to wear. However, the choice of suits was rather uninspiring and it took a long time before he found anything at all worthy of trying on. Testing the jacket for size, he found it a near perfect fit and then quickly retreated to a small changing room at the side to try on the pants.

"Okay, what do you think?" he asked Fayge as he emerged from the cubicle. "The jacket feels comfortable and the pants aren't too loose either."

Mrs. Klapman took careful stock of her husband in the black pinstriped suit before finally giving her approval.

"Yes, you're right," she confirmed. "It does look good on you. Excellent! Now all we've got to do is somehow or other find you a second suit, although judging from the selection here, it might not be such an easy task I'm afraid."

Fischel quickly changed back into his own clothes and was soon at his wife's side searching fervently for a second suit. However, the difficulty of this task could not be overstated. Many of the suits were long out of fashion and of rather obscure color and the few possible suits they tried either didn't fit correctly or were decidedly unflattering on Fischel's slim frame.

"Are you sure this brown one here is too light?" Fischel asked for the umpteenth time as he held aloft a yellow-tinged creation. "There isn't much else to choose from and I suppose it would do in an emergency."

Fayge, however, neglected to respond to this question, seeming unusually distracted from solving the second suit quandary.

"Fayge! I asked you something. Can you hear me?" pressed Fischel again. "Are you listening to me?"

But Fayge was not listening, as she made plainly apparent by an urgent gesticulation in his direction.

"SHHHHHHH!" she quietly insisted. "I don't want to miss this!"

Fischel looked quietly around for what had captured his wife's attention gradually tuning his ears into the interesting conversation taking place in the next aisle...............

ଔ ଔ ଔ

"Isn't this incredible Ari?" said Shuli to his friend. "Your new baby's four days old, you're making a Bris on Sunday and all you're doing is procrastinating over trying to get a free suit! If it's so important to you just take that black one over there with the red pin stripe which is certainly good enough for a second suit. Then we can get out of here already!"

"Can't you calm down and relax," Ari coaxed. "Choosing a suit takes time you know. I can't just rush into something because you've lost your patience."

"But we've been here for almost half an hour already!" whined Shuli. "How much more time are you going to need?"

"Shuli," said Ari patiently. "Let me explain something to you. You're twenty four years old now, right?"

"Right."

"Nice boy from a nice family, basically any nice girl's dream, right?"

"Okay."

"So why aren't you engaged or married yet?"

Shuli just stared dumbly as Ari continued with his explanation.

"Do you remember that girl you met just after Pesach? You were saying that even though everything seemed alright, you felt that it just didn't 'click'?"

"Okay, so what about it?"

"Well that's how I feel about this red pin-striped suit, ALRIGHT! Now if you'd just be a little more patient I'm sure I'll find something that I like."

By this time, Fischel and his wife had heard enough and both quickly rounded the end of the aisle rapidly closing in on Ari and Shuli. Fayge was about to step in and enquire more about Shuli's potential as a *shidduch* for her sister, but Fischel was quicker, pressing forth with his own agenda.

"Excuse me," he said interrupting their conversation, "But I couldn't help overhearing what you were saying. We've also been in this store for ages trying to find a second suit to take advantage of Mendy's offer and there really is nothing worthwhile. Maybe we could just buy our suits together and get one of them for free instead."

"Hey that's a great idea!" cried Shuli. "Ari, what do you say to this guy's offer? Looks like we can finally get out of here after all, no?"

Ari's towering and bulky figure looked down at Shuli and the Klapmans before replying.

"It might be," he said, "although I can't quite see Mendy agreeing to it. We couldn't even pretend to be the same size and there's no way Mendy will let us join together like that."

Fortunately Mendy had also been eavesdropping on the conversations in aisle three and was on hand to step in and put them at ease.

"Don't worry folks, it's okay," he interrupted. "You're right that normal store policy dictates the suits have to be the same size but you've both been here so long I'll be happy to make an exception. If you'll just come over to the sales counter I'll write up a bill and then we can complete the sale."

Grateful for this gesture the foursome followed dutifully behind Mendy as he marched through the aisles and up to the front of the store.

As he pulled ahead, there was just time enough for Ari to pop a quick question to Fischel.

"Were you intending to pay with cash or credit card?" he whispered as they walked up to pay.

"Cash actually."

"Okay that's good. I'll pay Mendy the total bill with my credit card and you can give me the cash afterwards. That way I can get the extra air miles. Would you mind at all?"

Fischel had no objections and allowed Ari to deal with Mendy directly while he stood and watched at a distance.

"How much is the total bill please?" Ari asked politely. "And I'll be paying with credit card if that's okay."

Mendy smiled back courteously.

"Well the size forty four is three hundred dollars and then you can take the two hundred dollar, thirty six regular for free. Credit card is fine."

The transaction was quickly completed and while Mendy busied himself wrapping the suits Fischel reached into his wallet for money to pay Ari. It didn't take long to extract the required bills and, as discreetly as he could, Fischel surreptitiously slipped Ari the money. Ari acknowledged the gesture but a closer look at what Fischel had handed over made him look a third time.

"Excuse me but you're fifty dollars short," he said to Fischel. "The total bill was actually three hundred dollars, not two hundred."

"Oh, that could be," replied Fischel, "but my suit was only priced at two hundred dollars. Half of that is one hundred dollars which is what I just gave you."

"No you're wrong," countered Ari. "You're meant to be paying a half of the total bill which works out to one hundred and fifty dollars. If you want to, you can go and choose a three hundred dollar suit to make sure you get your money's worth but anything less is just your loss."

Fischel furrowed his brow deep in thought knowing that something didn't sound right with Ari's reasoning.

"Sorry, but I think you're quite wrong," he finally challenged. "If I pay the same as you then we both own both suits. I own half of your suit and you own a half of mine. Now, if you want to take home my half of the three hundred dollar suit and leave us behind a two hundred dollar one then you'll have to pay for that privilege."

This logical challenge caught Ari quite off guard and he had no idea how to respond.

"Shuli, do you have any idea what this guy wants?" he finally asked his friend. "I just don't see what the problem is."

Shuli though was similarly unable to shed any clarity on the situation and eventually the bickering and snapping reached Mendy's ears. He found the exchange slightly disconcerting especially as it was taking place in his store.

"Perhaps I could suggest," he interjected, clearing his throat, "that you split the cost of the extra fifty dollars and that Mr. Klapman pay just twenty five dollars extra instead of the full fifty to make you both happy?"

☞ *Whose solution- Fischel's, Ari's or Mendy's, is the Halachically correct one? (p. 241)*

15

A Deathbed Gambit

It was just before Shabbos when the call from New York came in.

"Abba's very sick," Daniel Harari heard Moshe, his half-brother say. "I think you and Ezra should come as soon as possible."

Further details were not necessary. Even from his home far away in Jerusalem, Daniel knew well the precarious situation of his ailing father's health. So severe was Rachamim's situation, the phone call had almost been inevitable in coming.

After nightfall the next day Daniel and Ezra set about getting to New York as quickly as possible. Cost was of no object. The urgency of the call had made sure of that and in any event the Harari family fortune would more than cover the expense. Twin first-class tickets were soon procured and within hours the brothers were speeding their way towards Ben-Gurion International Airport in a private limousine.

Life had not always been so easy for the Harari family. In fact there had once been a time when a lack of money had been the least of their problems.

ଓ ଓ ଓ

It could just as well have been a leisurely afternoon stroll. Rachamim Harari and his two sons casually sauntered their way towards the town square well aware of the enormity of their actions. For this was Arabia in the late 1940's when there was almost no reprieve from the cruel regime's battle to uproot religion from the infidels. Especially endangered by new legislation were the teenage Harari brothers for whom an army draft was an imminent reality.

And so Rachamim had planned for his boys to have their only chance of true freedom- ESCAPE! A taxi from the town square was to take them to the next village where they were to board a bus traveling north towards the border territories. From there, a paid scout was to take them on a three-day hike over the treacherous mountains and across the border to freedom.

But the risk of the authorities discovering their scheme was ever-present and Rachamim could do no more than bid his sons the most casual of farewells, his churning emotions buried deep beneath his painted smile.

With the departure of the taxi Rachamim paused for the briefest of moments before returning towards what was now the shadow of his former home. Having been widowed a decade earlier he had since then devoted all his energies to raising his sons, an effort which had now culminated in that day's events.

Bereft and alone, Rachamim was equally struck by the very real fear for his children's present circumstances and physical safety. Had he done the right thing? Was it really correct to rely on half-truths from money-hungry, unscrupulous smugglers? Was there really no other choice than to send the boys away?

Such tortuous thoughts and contemplation could well have driven Rachamim insane had it not been for his very good friend who knew precisely what Rachamim would be going through. For not more than five minutes after his return home was there a knock on the door from the indefatigable Moshe Farzani. Sluggishly, Rachamim rose from his seat of despondence to answer the door.

"Oh, Moshe it's you," said Rachamim upon seeing who was on the doorstep. "I suppose you'd better come in." Rachamim turned and shuffled back to a chair in the living room beckoning his friend to follow suit. Moshe needed no encouragement and was soon seated comfortably next to his close friend.

"Rammy, listen to me well," said Moshe getting straight down to business. "Now that your boys have gone it's high time you began thinking of yourself again."

"Why? I mean what do you mean?" Rachamim asked.

"I'm referring to my sister-in-law," explained Moshe. "She has waited for you long enough and the least you could do for both yourself and her is to consider the match."

The suddenness of this proclamation paralyzed Rachamim into stunned silence but he soon regained his composure, replying with the mantra he had invoked so often before.

"Moshe, I'm far too old to get married again," he objected. "I'll just try and survive until I can find a way to get out of this country and get back together again with my boys."

This time however the inane age-objection held little sway over a seasoned matchmaker the likes of Moshe. Forcefully and fluently, he eloquently presented one convincing argument after another until finally Rachamim had relented and agreed to meet Bolisa.

As Moshe had predicted, the two were amicably compatible and within a week of their first meeting the *shidduch* was already being announced. A year later the welcome birth of their infant son Moshe made the *simcha* complete.

It was many years before the Harari family (mark II) were also able to escape that oppressive regime, eventually making their way to the shores of America. After settling in the Brooklyn section of New York, Rachamim opened a small carpet business which soon prospered and diversified considerably, making the family quite wealthy indeed.

Alas, Rachamim's anticipation of enduring tranquility and a happy and comfortable retirement were not to be realized. A routine visit to the doctor uncovered a potentially dangerous health condition mandating a range of unsettling treatments and therapies. The diagnosis of Bolisa's own sickness compounded his suffering yet further and with her untimely passing merely months later it seemed as if his own lease on life would itself end prematurely. Indeed, had it not been for his children's constant care and concern he could well have given up on his own fight for life.

☙ ☙ ☙

The arrival of their plane in New York roused Daniel and Ezra from these contemplative thoughts to attend to the immediate calling of completing their journey. Without stowed luggage they soon exited through customs and immigration, and continued speedily on their way to their father's hospital.

The situation looked extremely grave at Rachamim's bedside. He lay still and quiet, the numerous tubes and wires hooked up to his body portraying the dismal picture of a very sick man indeed.

"He almost hasn't moved at all today," reported Moshe, "and the doctors really think it's only a matter of time now."

The vigil began that same evening with Daniel staying up the entire night allowing Ezra a few precious hours to rest and recover from the flight. The next morning Ezra took over while Moshe kept himself constantly busy ensuring his brothers' immediate needs were amply met.

Alas, this scenario only lasted for little more than thirty-six hours. Late on Monday evening the urgent electronic screeching of a heart monitor hurriedly summoned the nurses to the room where Rachamim lay. They sought to quickly stabilize his condition but alas, despite their alacrity there was really naught to be done. A few weeks short of his seventy-second birthday Rachamim Harari's soul had departed this fleeting, temporal world in search of a better place in a different dimension.

Moshe had taken care to prime the *chevra kadisha* in advance of their father's circumstances and they were almost instantly on hand to help deal with Rachamim's final arrangements. Burial took place the very next day and subsequently the three sons sat down to observe *shiva* together in the family home. They used the time well, reminiscing over the past while simultaneously strengthening their bonds for the future. However, this peace and tranquility lasted only until a meeting the following week in the law offices of Messrs. Alistair Bushwood and Co.

"Welcome, welcome please come and sit down," said Mr. Bushwood eagerly. "You must be Daniel and Ezra, correct?" he added nodding in the direction of the Israeli branch of the family. "Yes, I've heard much about you from your brother these past few weeks haven't I Mo?" he continued with a sly snicker, as he glanced back to Moshe.

This quite unnerved Daniel and Ezra who were none too thrilled at having their father's *impartial* attorney so chummy with their half-brother Nonetheless, now was not the time for petty concerns.

"Yes, that's correct," confirmed Daniel. "Now if you please, could you get on with the business at hand and skip the formalities. We do have a lot to attend to at home and would appreciate it if you could get a move on with things."

"But of course sir whatever you wish," replied the smug attorney. "It'll be my pleasure. In fact, if you're so rushed for time you'll really appreciate the brevity of your father's last wishes."

With this rather ominous sounding introduction, Mr. Bushwood opened the file on his desk, extracted a single sheet, cleared his throat with a rather deliberate-sounding cough and began in the most professional of voices he could muster.

"I, Rachamim Harari being of sound mind, wish the following directives to be adhered to in the eventuality of my death. Be it known that in lieu of the variation and complexity of my different investments I see it fit to bequeath two million dollars each to my sons Daniel and Ezra, the remainder of my estate to be given to my son Moshe."

Daniel and Ezra waited breath for some continuation or clarification, but that was it. Bushwood had finished speaking.

Now to the uninitiated two million dollars may have sounded like a sizeable sum but Daniel and Ezra knew better. Their father had held shares and investments in a variety of conglomerates, commercial banking and entrepreneurial schemes and while Daniel did not have an exact figure of his father's net worth he at least knew that four million dollars between him and Ezra was a paltry sum indeed. Too paltry in fact and certainly in dire need of further investigation.

"Excuse me sir," demanded Daniel from the attorney. "Can I inspect that document myself please? What you just read out bears no relation at all to what Abba has been telling us for years about how he would hand down his possessions."

Dutifully, Mr. Bushwood submitted a copy of the will to Daniel and another to Ezra allowing them both to verify for themselves the authenticity of the document. Daniel was the first to voice an objection.

"I don't understand," he blurted out. "The date on this will is February the twenty seventh. That was only ten days ago. In fact," he added checking his calendar, "that was the Sunday that we arrived here from Israel. There is no way that Abba was in a fit state at that point to draft a will. This must be a forgery!"

Moshe turned to the lawyer for clarification.

"Not at all, Mr. Harari," explained Alistair Bushwood, LLC. "It was actually quite late on Saturday evening when your brother called me to the hospital to meet with your late father. Certainly the elderly man was very weak at that time but it was clearly explained to him that amending the will would actually be in everyone's best interest. Practically speaking Mr. Harari you must agree that to quantify and assign a monetary value to *all* of your late father's holdings would be a tremendous task in of itself. Rather than tying up all the assets until such a report could be completed- which could take years, it was deemed preferable to simply assign cash monies to the overseas members of the family and leave your brother here with the headache of processing and transferring the assets to his name. You must agree after all Mr. Harari that two million dollars cash *is* a fine sum indeed, wouldn't you say so?"

"I can't believe this!" exclaimed Ezra. "This must be a mistake! Even if this is my father's signature he must have been duped into signing. There's just no way he could have wantonly altered his will so drastically at the last moment."

"I'm afraid you are quite mistaken Mr. Harari," corrected Bushwood, "and that everything was indeed carried out according to protocol. In actual fact when the idea of the change was presented to your father he even suggested calling you to confirm the change but you were already on the airplane at that time and not reachable."

"I don't believe a word of it!" exclaimed Ezra to Daniel. "It's a put-up job. It must be!"

"Come, come sir," said Bushwood patronizingly. "That's a very grave accusation to make regarding your late father's final wishes. For your information the counter-signatures of the resident doctor and nurse who were present at the time well attest that Mr. Harari was indeed of sound mind when the document was signed and sealed."

Daniel and Ezra were completely speechless at the seemingly organized crime that had been executed against their interests. However, it seemed that Moshe's scheme had been well thought-out and orchestrated indeed.

"So would you like your two million in a cash payment here, or would you like to have it wired to an account abroad or something similar?" Bushwood asked again.

"NEITHER!" exploded Daniel. "I'm not going to settle for a paltry two million without hammering this out in Beit Din. Come on Ezra!" he said turning to his full brother. "Let's get out of here. I don't want to spend another minute with this crook!"

Moshe, however, was quite unfazed by Daniel's forceful showing.

"You can shout and yell all you want," he said back heatedly, "but it won't help. Abba's signature is all that we need and there is no way you'll successfully challenge this in any *Beit Din* at all."

☞ *Can Daniel and Ezra salvage any more than two million dollars each from their late father's fifty million dollar estate? (p. 243)*

16

Appliance Agony

It was a ten-year-old Peretz Weissbaum that stood and looked up at the huge gates of Charlie Murphy's scrap metal yard. Through them he gazed across a sculpted landscape of worn out bicycles, doorless refrigerators and an enormous collection of ancient automobiles. Presently a huge metal crane came down upon an old Pontiac Station wagon its claws clasping together through the car's dented doors and broken windows. This was in fact no ordinary car but one that had been a part of Peretz's family for as long as he could remember. Through waves of nostalgia, he watched as the car was lifted high into the air and swung around to where a huge hydraulic metal crusher lay empty, eagerly awaiting its next feast. With the car in place two heavy metal plates slowly closed in on each other, inexorably crushing the car, and Peretz's spirit along with it.

As the sounds of buckling metal and aromas of burning oil slowly entered an adult Peretz's fuddled subconscious mind, he realized his daydream into the past had exceeded its accepted boundaries. Wresting himself anxiously from the armchair he darted into the kitchen where he soon discovered the very real source of these disquieting tones and odors.

"Pessy!" he called out desperately to his wife. "Come quickly! Look what's happening with the *fleishige* dishwasher."

Pessy ran quickly into the kitchen just in time to hear the old machine give a final grunt before becoming eternally silent.

"I think it's broken down," she said perceptively as the reality of what had transpired began to sink in. The two of them stood there together for a few minutes deep in thought, each drawing strength from the other during this trying period. Finally Pessy broke the silence.

"Oh, well! I guess this had to be expected at some point. After all, the machine *was* almost twenty years old."

"Well what are we to do now?" asked Peretz helplessly.

"I'll wash and you can dry," said Pessy firmly, recovering from the initial shock, "and then we can go out together and buy a new machine!"

Although typically the more frugal of the two, Pessy's determined tone made it clear how important it was to her to have the dishwasher replaced. Whether he liked it or not, Peretz would have to somehow or other find the funds to cover the purchase.

The display of dishwashers in Silvermans Electronics Store was both impressive and confusing. Some of the machines looked very similar but had very different price tags while others seemed to boast of programs and features that Peretz and Pessy had never imagined or heard of previously. Before they became completely bamboozled by the selection Shimon Silverman CEO stepped in to offer his assistance and advice.

"Good evening and welcome to our store," he began in his friendly, trademark manner. "As you can see we have a wonderful selection of the latest model dishwashers all priced to sell. What can I help you with today?" he asked encouragingly.

"Basically we need a new dishwasher," Peretz began, taking the lead. "We had our old one for twenty years but it just broke down and I guess it needs replacing."

"Well you've come to the right place then," replied Shimon putting a more upbeat air on their dialogue. "Each of the models you see here do just a marvelous job of cleaning food and grime from dirty plates, each in its own unique way. Perhaps if you'd give me an idea of the color you'd like and how much you're looking to spend I could help narrow down the search and assist you in making an informed decision."

Shimon listened attentively as Peretz and Pessy described what they were looking for, punctuating their narrative with a few accurately placed questions. Finally, after a few minutes, Shimon was ready to make his recommendations.

"I think you'd be best off with something from the Yurmukoff range of machines," he suggested. "They offer simple, one-touch operation, have excellent racks for the largest of dishes and also incorporate the latest in energy saving technology."

Shimon then directed Peretz and Pessy towards a machine stacked neatly towards the rear of the display. They opened it up and had a good look at the interior while Shimon continued with his presentation. "All the models I have in mind come in this same basic design. This one here, model number YMK two three seven two four offers a choice of five different programs in four different modes, and comes with a host of other features as standard. The next model up, the YMK two four seven three four offers all this plus the benefits of an added cycle, delayed start and a water saving setting. However, I would also suggest you consider the YMK three seven two four three XT deluxe model. It does cost slightly more than the figure you mentioned, but with multiple settings, a whisper-quiet motor and superlative pot-cleaning power it really is worth considering," he said, ending with a flair.

"Well I'm not interested in spending so much on a machine," Peretz replied without hesitation, "so that model is definitely out. Now exactly what kind of price are we talking about for the other two machines."

"I'm glad you asked that," replied Shimon confidently. "Right now the basic model is selling for three hundred and ninety five dollars, but we have a special on the two four seven three four. That normally retails for five hundred and twenty five, but today, after discounts and rebates it can be yours for only four hundred and fifty five."

Although the deal sounded good Peretz preferred to spend conservatively and decline the improved performance promised in the upgraded more expensive machine. At least, he figured, a new machine however basic would be infinitely better than the broken one sitting in their kitchen at home.

This satisfaction turned to pleasure and delight with the arrival and subsequent use of their new dishwasher. Compared to their old model, the new Yurmukoff was a refreshing change, processing the dishes more quickly, cleanly and quietly than ever before. Peretz himself took particular delight in their new purchase and he would often take a recreational stroll into the kitchen after dinner just to watch and listen to the machine in action.

This, however was strictly an evening activity, the mornings being a quite different story. After breakfast, it was the *milchige* dishwasher their kitchen had to contend with and although it performed with a reasonable degree of efficiency it in no way compared to the new *fleishige* Yurmukoff. After one particularly noisy cycle Peretz presented his qualms over the machine to Pessy.

"What would you say to a new *milchige* dishwasher?" he asked her enthusiastically. "Don't you think the one we have is really past it already?"

Pessy was not so inclined to agree albeit for slightly different reasons.

"Peretz, you know I'm always in favor of replacing things before they break," she explained, "but to be honest, have we finished paying for the new *fleishige* one yet? There's still a balance on the credit card, and with the *milchige* machine still basically doing its job, now's not the time to splurge on a replacement."

Peretz could not deny the validity of her argument - there was indeed some money still owed on the credit card but with Pessy's birthday approaching he felt determined to at least try and do something.

It was difficult. The family budget was rather tight, but with some economizing measures over the next few weeks and a stroke of good fortune at work Peretz managed to squirrel away enough to cover the cost of a new machine. With cash in hand, he boldly made his way towards Silvermans Electronics Store where he was met once again by an ebullient Shimon Silverman.

"Good morning sir and welcome to our store. What can I help you with today?"

"Well actually I was here last month when we bought a new dishwasher and........"

"Certainly, now I remember," interrupted Shimon. "It was a new Yurmukoff right? You were here then with your wife if I'm not mistaken."

"That's exactly right," confirmed Peretz. "In fact, we're so delighted with it, I've come to buy another one."

"Another one?" asked Shimon slightly confused.

"Yes," confirmed Peretz. "We were so happy with the new *fleishige* one we decided to replace the *milchige* one also. To tell you the truth actually," he said leaning closer, "it's actually meant to be a surprise for my wife. You see, it's her birthday next Tuesday and if you could arrange for delivery on that day it would be just wonderful."

"Certainly sir! Next Tuesday would be no problem at all," confirmed Shimon. "Now do you remember exactly which machine it was so we can place the order?"

"Yes, it was the Yurmukoff two three something or other and it cost three hundred and ninety five dollars," volunteered Peretz. "Does that help you?"

Shimon paused momentarily to digest the information before finally responding.

"I think I know the machine you are referring to," he said tactfully, "but I'll just go and pull up your original record from last time to make sure we get the correct machine."

Shimon retreated back to a computerized sales platform where he was able to quickly retrieve Peretz's previous sales invoice.

"I see now the machine you got," he confirmed. "As it happens that model has actually gone up in price by thirty dollars since you were last here," he added taking careful note of Peretz's demeanor, "but in recognition of your good custom I'll still hold it at the original price. Would that be okay?"

"Absolutely fine," confirmed Peretz, grateful for Shimon's money-saving gesture. "Now about that delivery date..."

"Next Tuesday you said, wasn't it?" interrupted Shimon. "That's the nineteenth if I'm not mistaken. Now would you prefer morning or afternoon?"

"Morning I think," replied Peretz. "That would be just the thing to get her day off to a good start."

"Excellent! I couldn't agree more," confirmed Shimon. "I'm sure your wife will be most appreciative of such a thoughtful gift."

"I'm sure she will too," said Peretz, gleefully imagining Pessy's delighted reaction with the surprise delivery.

His imagination was not wrong. Just before noon that following Tuesday, Pessy, answered the unfamiliar knocking at the front door, subconsciously aware there existed the potential for a birthday surprise.

The deliveryman had been tipped off well and with a broad grin wished her a happy birthday and preceded to bring in the large box containing the new machine. Under her excited eye the box and all its wrappings were carefully removed until the gift sat before her in all its glory.

"A new dishwasher!" she exclaimed, clasping her hands together in unbridled, delighted joy.

"Yes ma'am, a new dishwasher," confirmed Bruno, the deliveryman. "Now, where would you like it installed. It says something on my instructions about a milkik side."

"Of course, of course. That would be right over here near the window," she explained showing where the old *milchige* machine lay.

It took Bruno but a few short minutes to connect the new machine and as the delivery truck drove off with the old dishwasher, Pessy was already on the phone to Peretz expressing her gratitude.

"And you needn't worry about any credit card bills either," he told her reassuringly. "Your new machine has already been paid for in full!"

Pleased that his birthday surprise had cheered Pessy so, Peretz spent the remainder of his day in elevated spirits, quickly and efficiently dealing with all the tasks that crossed his work desk that afternoon.

Alas, his joy lasted only as long as it took him to arrive home that evening. Strolling into the kitchen to inspect the new machine was quite enough to shake his joyful demeanor.

"I don't understand," he said puzzledly as he spied the new machine. "This isn't the one I ordered."

"It isn't?" asked Pessy.

"No it isn't at all," confirmed Peretz. "I ordered another one like the fleishige one we got. This one looks a lot more basic to me."

"Well, it not only looks inferior," added Pessy. "It certainly doesn't do nearly as good a job either. And it sounded just as noisy as our old one also."

"I can't believe this!" said Peretz slapping his forehead. "How could they have sent us the wrong model? We'll just have to call them in the morning and have it corrected."

ଓ ଓ ଓ

"You say you were shipped the wrong model?" Shimon asked incredulously that next morning as he took Peretz's phone call. "That's terrible! Give me an hour or two to investigate and I'll get back to you as soon as I have more information."

With those few words, Shimon was able to temporarily placate Peretz as he set about trying to solve the mystery. However, try as he may he could not figure out where the problem lay. The sales order number matched with the warehouse release code which similarly matched the model number on the dishwasher Peretz had ordered a month earlier.

"Mr. Weissbaum, are you sure it's not the correct model?" Shimon pressed him again on the phone later that day. "I've checked everything and can't seem to find a discrepancy anywhere. Maybe the error is on your part after all?"

Naturally Peretz was not at all satisfied with this response maintaining that he had been sorely treated with the incorrect delivery of an inferior machine.

"Well something is not right that's for certain," he insisted, "and you can even come round and see for yourself!"

Both out of curiosity and a keen sense of customer goodwill Shimon acquiesced to Peretz's offer, arranging to meet later that evening.

"Your address is not far from where I live, and I can make a point of stopping by on my way to Maariv. Will that be okay?"

Peretz confirmed this was in order and began preparing himself for what he perceived would be a major showdown later on.

ꝏ ꝏ ꝏ

At a quarter to eight Shimon arrived at Peretz's door and was soon ushered into the kitchen where the unwanted dishwasher lay. Taking his time Shimon made a careful inspection making sure the controls were all working correctly and the installation done properly.

"Well everything seems to be in order," he finally said straightening his knees from a crouched position, "but wait one second!" he suddenly called, his eyes taking in the rest of the kitchen. "What on earth is that over there?"

Peretz followed his gaze away from the window not sure as to the cause of Shimon's surprise.

"That? Why, that's the *fleishige* dishwasher we bought from you last month," replied Peretz flatly. "Why do you ask?"

Shimon didn't reply but instead walked slowly over for a closer look.

"It can't be!" said Shimon, making his inspection. "It just can't be!"

"Wha.....What can't be?" pressed Peretz, concerned at Shimon's unusual interest in the machine. "You sold it to us yourself. Is...is there a problem with it?"

"Problem?! Problem?! I'll say there's a problem! This machine here is a top-of-the-line Yurmukoff XT deluxe model! How on earth did you end up with this here?"

"Your people delivered it," replied Peretz now totally confused. "Just like they did this cheap *milchige* one over here. Can you believe it?"

But Shimon wasn't listening, instead simply letting his fingers run over the machine again and again as his mind worked feverishly in an attempt to solve the mystery.

"Mr. Weissbaum, I don't know how this could have happened," he finally said, "but the trouble isn't with your new *milchige* dishwasher. That one's absolutely fine and just what you ordered and paid for. The problem is with your *fleishige* dishwasher. Somehow or other this deluxe model was shipped to you instead of the basic model you just got now."

"So what do you want me to do about it?" asked Peretz worriedly.

Shimon sighed.

"Nothing I guess. I suppose you just got lucky. I'm not going to charge you the difference."

"Very good then," replied Peretz somewhat relieved. "Now how about this cheap *milchige* one. It's not at all what we want. We'd much rather the fancier one if you have it available."

Pleased that his customer now seemed happy again, Shimon reverted back to his salesman's demeanor, eager to please and even more eager to complete a sale.

"Certainly sir! We'll arrange for an emergency delivery for you tomorrow morning," replied Shimon. "Obviously I'll waive any return charge and I'll give you a full credit for the price of this machine. Will that be okay?"

"Sounds good," replied Peretz. "This machine is really not what we want at all."

"Excellent!" replied Shimon, pleased he had made the sale. "I'll arrange for COD for the balance for the new machine which you can give the driver when he comes."

While this response had been said quite matter-of-factly, Shimon's subtle inference had not been lost on Peretz.

"The balance?" repeated Peretz. "What kind of balance? I thought you were giving me full credit for the machine since it was your fault we received it in error."

"Of course we'll give you full credit," explained Shimon reassuringly. "Although the machine has been used I guess it wasn't your fault. Now I'm not sure off-hand exactly how much more the deluxe model is - probably around three hundred dollars or so but if you call the store in the morning I'll give you an exact figure then."

"WHAT DID YOU SAY?" cried Peretz in near shock. "AROUND THREE HUNDRED DOLLARS! I'm not spending that kind of money extra on a new dishwasher. I thought you'd just be able to make a straight swap because it's really your fault altogether, and I don't have any more money to give you anyway."

"No, I don't think you understand," Shimon tried explaining again. "I'm only taking this machine back as a courtesy. Ordinarily once a machine has been delivered and installed I don't accept any returns and it's only because of the confusion that I feel obligated to accommodate you. However, if you want the deluxe model I will have to charge you standard showroom price." On this Shimon was quite firm and clearly not willing to negotiate.

"But what if I can't afford the extra money?" Peretz whined. "Then what do I do?"

"Well you always have the option of simply keeping the model you have. It may not be the deluxe model you had intended, but it still does the job of cleaning your dishes which is ultimately what you want, isn't it?"

Peretz shrugged his shoulders in dull agreement. Spending more money on a new machine was simply not an option and it seemed he would have to make do with the cheaper Yurmukoff.

"One second though," he said, thinking out loud. "This machine you've sold me is really no better than the old one I was replacing and quite frankly a complete waste of the four hundred dollars I already gave you. In that case I'd like to return it and just get my money back instead."

Shimon had not been prepared for this request, but found himself cornered. Peretz did after all have a valid claim in that he had never intended to purchase a base model machine and maybe really was entitled to his money back. Feeling somewhat defeated, Shimon resigned himself to the loss and informed a grateful Peretz that he would grant him a full refund on the new but unwanted machine.

"But remember I don't want it used again," cautioned Shimon. "And certainly if it gets scratched at all or damaged I won't be able to make the return and you'll be left with it."

"Okay sir, that sounds fair," agreed Peretz, and the two men shook hands on the arrangement expressing their mutual consent.

଒ ଒ ଒

It was the following evening when the Silverman appliance truck returned to the Weissbaum home. Peretz himself rose to answer the knocking at the door.

"Good evening sir, we're here for the dishwasher," said Bruno who was back again for the pick-up. "Can we come in please?"

Peretz stood aside to let Bruno and his subordinate through and watched as they made their own way into the kitchen. They made straight for the *milchige* dishwasher, expertly disconnected it and then carried it out of the kitchen, through the front door and onto their truck outside. However, before they managed to drive off Peretz realized there had been an apparent, glaring omission.

"One second," he called out to the driver, as he ran frantically across his front lawn. "Where's our old machine? You're meant to bring it back now also," he maintained. "You are the same crew that delivered this one by mistake on Tuesday, aren't you?"

"Yes we are," confirmed the driver, "but I don't think we can really help you with your old machine."

"Why not?" asked Peretz. "Just bring it back and then reconnect the hoses. It shouldn't take more than a few minutes."

While Peretz looked towards the driver in anticipation of some more quick service, he was totally unprepared for the shocking blow that was about to come. Indeed, even as the driver spoke, Peretz's entire body was engulfed in the neurotic trauma from years gone by.

"Your old machine?" said the driver. "Oh, no sir! We already took that over to Charlie Murphy's place."

☞ *Is Shimon responsible for the unwanted disposal of The Weissbaum's milchige dishwasher? (p. 245)*

☞ *Would Shimon have been allowed to charge the Weissbaums the higher price for the first dishwasher? (ibid)*

17

Exercise and Caution

The *Beis Hamedrash* walls sang forth with the familiar, mesmerizing clamor of intense *Torah* learning. Forwards and back the arguments flew, each more energized than the next as the young men sparred with each other in furious debate.

"It's obvious that Reuven has to pay Shimon," insisted Yehoshua. "When he hired him to work, he was guaranteeing Shimon his wages for that day."

"Yeah, but it wasn't Reuven's fault that some other guy showed up and did the job instead, so why should he pay him for not doing anything?"

And so it continued hour after hour through the course of the afternoon. Then, as if guided by an unseen hand, the *kollel* members simultaneously and abruptly ended their learning session.

"Hey Nachman, it's already seven o'clock," Yehoshua said quickly to his friend. "We'd better get running if we're going to catch the tender home."

Grabbing his hat and jacket Yehoshua flew off down the block towards the bus with Nachman behind struggling unsuccessfully to keep up. So much so that Yehoshua was already settled comfortably when an exhausted Nachman climbed aboard the bus and flopped down into an adjacent seat.

"Yehoshua, you've gotta slow down for me next time," he managed to blurt out between desperate gasps for air. "I'm not as young as you and just can't keep up with your energy."

Yehoshua looked at his friend puzzledly.

"Nachman, you're only one year older than me," he pointedly noted, "and it's nothing to do with age. Just simply that you're out of shape."

Nachman nodded slowly without bothering to verbalize an acknowledgement; his labored breathing more than testified to the fact.

"Well you've really got to start doing something about it then," encouraged Yehoshua. "Like losing weight and more importantly getting regular exercise."

"You're really right," agreed Nachman. "I should exercise more, but what can I do? It's just my lifestyle I guess. We're not all as fortunate as you to own our own fancy elliptical orbiter you know."

Yehoshua pondered this wishful comment thoughtfully before responding.

"You're right!" he confirmed. "Having the orbiter is convenient but listen to this. How would you like to borrow it for a few months?"

Nachman was puzzled.

"What? Borrow your orbiter? How do you mean?"

"I mean borrow it," repeated Yehoshua. "How would you like to borrow it for a few months. Like from now until after Succos."

"Well……… I mean like… why do you ask? Don't you use it yourself?"

Yehoshua laughed.

"Sure! Every day for twenty minutes! But that's not the point. It's just that we're going back home in a few weeks and we'll probably be there until the beginning of winter. My wife's due to have a baby mid-October and we reckoned that since she'd want to be home for the baby we might as well spend Ellul there also. So if we're away you might as well use the machine, rather than have it sit around our apartment doing nothing. Think you'd want it? It's very light and portable and would be no trouble for you to bring round."

"I…I don't know what to tell you," replied a stunned Nachman. "Forget about that orbiter thing! I can't believe you're leaving us just like that."

"Well, that's just the way it's worked out, I guess," explained Yehoshua sounding rather resigned. "But it's only for three months and really isn't such a big deal if you think about it."

This said, Yehoshua turned contemplatively to take in the passing Jerusalem scenery, a sentiment keenly noticed by his friend.

"You're not going to come back, you know that," Nachman warned with quiet authority. "There's just no way that after three months away you're going to pick yourselves up again to come back, and with a new baby too. It just doesn't happen."

"No way!" replied Yehoshua forcefully. "We're both really happy here and determined to come back. In fact, if my mother-in-law weren't so insistent we'd probably have stayed here for the baby in the first place!"

"I'm glad to hear it!" said Nachman. "Too many good guys ended up staying in America after going back for a baby. Anyhow," he continued, "I'm not sure what to tell you about the orbiter but let me run it past my wife and see what she thinks."

To say Yael Hoffman was excited at the thought of possessing an elliptical orbiter exerciser would be the most extreme of understatements. Well aware of her husband's expanding girth and resultant decreased energy, the potential benefits of having exercise equipment instantly available on their own premises were too great to ignore. Nonetheless, she remained as selfless as ever, thinking only of the good of her potential benefactors.

"That's very nice of your *chavrusah* to make such an offer but it sounds a bit strange to me," she commented thoughtfully. "If they're leaving for the summer and not coming back until after Succos then why would they want to keep their apartment altogether! They'll be paying three months rent for nothing!"

"I don't know- maybe to make sure they'll come back afterwards," reasoned Nachman, "although it does sound like a rather expensive way of doing things."

"Expensive?" repeated Yael. "It'd be a dreadful waste of money! Maybe I should call Devorah and see if we can sort this thing out? It just doesn't make any sense, paying three months rent like that for nothing."

True to her word, Yael called Devorah Greenstein that very next morning and expressed her concerns

"I heard you're leaving for a while Devorah," Yael began. "It'll be such a shame not to have you around. But what's this about your exercise machine that your husband mentioned to Nachman yesterday?"

"I think that Yehoshua just thought it would be a nice idea to lend it to you while we were away. Do you think you'd want it?"

"Yes, but that's not the point. I was more concerned about the rest of your things. What would you be doing with them while you're away?"

"I guess we'll just leave them in the apartment until we get back. That should be safe enough don't you think?"

"Possibly," replied Yael not so sure it would be, "but then you'll then be paying rent for all the months you're not here which would be a terrible waste. Why not just move out and look for a new apartment when you get back? You'll need a second bedroom anyway, what with a new baby so there's really no reason to hold on to the apartment you have now."

Yael's argument did ring true in Devorah's ears but there was one concern it failed to address.

"That's all very well," she confirmed, "but what will we do with all our things while we're away. We can't exactly take them back with us. Did you think about that?"

"Well that's exactly why I'm calling," exclaimed Yael. "Your furniture isn't your own, isn't it?" she asked.

"No it's not actually. It came with the apartment."

"Good! Now if that's the case you could just leave all of your things with us! Our second bedroom is very roomy and we've place in there for far more than just an exercise machine. You might think it's not worth the trouble packing everything up but I'm sure once it's done you'd feel much happier rather than having everything sit in an empty apartment."

"Yael, that is so kind of you to offer," replied Devorah. "We really don't want to start imposing on anyone while we're away but maybe I'll bring it up with my husband later when he gets home."

Yehoshua's initial reaction was also one of selfless independence and that they should keep their apartment. Nonetheless, the considerable financial savings being suggested did merit giving the matter more serious thought.

"I suppose it shouldn't be too much work to pack everything up," Yehoshua said, his eyes scanning the apartment in taking stock of their possessions. "We've still got nearly three weeks before we leave and if I get hold of some boxes tomorrow that should be plenty of time to pack up everything."

Devorah, despite her expectant state, agreed that the idea seemed quite workable being simultaneously relieved their belongings would not be left in an empty apartment during their absence. Sturdy cardboard boxes were soon procured and the packing started shortly thereafter in earnest.

It was two and a half weeks later that twenty-seven neatly packaged cardboard boxes arrived into the Hoffman's apartment together with the much lauded after elliptical orbiter.

"That's twenty minutes a day, no less," Yael instructed her husband after the Greensteins had left. "It seems to have worked wonders for your friend and there's no reason you shouldn't build up your strength the same way. After all, there's no sense having this thing sitting around if we're not going to make the most of it."

"Don't worry, I certainly intend to make good use of it," replied Nachman reassuringly. "Especially with *bein Hazmanim* coming up, it'll certainly keep me busy."

ଓ ଓ ଓ

It is a well-known axiom that the joyful anticipation of any given activity is inversely proportional to the actual joy engendered from that pursuit. It is similarly well known that any cost-benefit analysis decision requires constant monitoring to ensure the costs and benefits of the study retain their relative values ensuring the continued efficacy of the original decision. This is especially relevant in the realm of exercise equipment which is wont to lose its utility value rather rapidly.

It is perhaps not as well known that twenty seven boxes of another's personal effects and possessions stuffed into the corner of one's sole spare bedroom can seem to grow and expand exponentially over time, occupying a larger and larger space. Such was the gradual discovery of Nachman and Yael Hoffman throughout the summer and Ellul, and even the joyous news of a new Greenstein arrival shortly after Succos did little to shrink the growing nuisance in their minds.

"You'll see," commented Nachman to his wife. "They're probably going to stay now for the *Bris,* then for the *Pidyon Haben* and then for Chanukah and by that time they'll stay for good and we'll be left with all their junk!"

"Don't be such a pessimist!" rebuked Yael. "I'm sure they'll be back sooner than you imagine. I know the boxes are a bit in the way but Devorah did insist they were absolutely coming back."

Despite this assurance Nachman remained skeptical and determined to find out for himself if Yehoshua was indeed planning an imminent return. Through a series of discreet enquiries and surreptitious, clandestine detective work, Nachman's perseverance bore fruit and one joyous afternoon he became privy to some prized and vital information which he gleefully shared with Yael.

"Great news!" he announced upon his arrival home. "You were right! Yehoshua, Devorah and Junior Greenstein *are* coming back soon and will actually be moving into an apartment on the third floor of the next building."

"Next door?" she repeated pleasantly surprised. "That's so nice. When are they arriving?"

"In about three weeks but listen to this! Three weeks from now is the middle of December but they're going to have to take the apartment from the first. That means we could begin dumping off all their stuff as soon as the end of next week. "

"Are you sure that's a good idea?" asked Yael doubtfully, not sharing her husband's gleeful enthusiasm. "Shouldn't we wait until they're back for sure?"

"What's better," continued Nachman not listening, "is that I even know where to get hold of the key. Don't you think it would be nice for them to arrive back and find all their boxes already returned?"

"Possibly," replied Yael still unsure, "but tell me, how on earth did you find out all this information?"

Nachman shrugged modestly.

"Devorah's brother just told me on the way home from *shul*."

☙ ☙ ☙

Monday 17th December 2007
33 R'chov ben Zundel, Jerusalem

"WELCOME BACK!" proclaimed a colorfully decorated sign upon the door of apartment number eleven, a most heartwarming gesture to greet three wearied Greenstein travelers. Opening the door, Yehoshua and Devorah gratefully discovered some of the other kind preparations that had been made in advance of their return-the beds were neatly made, basic foodstuffs were on the table and even their boxes of possessions had been kindly returned. In fact, it was perhaps this latter gesture that was to prove the most useful. The effects of jet lag coupled with a new baby ensured Yehoshua and Devorah slept little that night providing them with ample time to put their lives back in order.

Nostalgically, Devorah unpacked one box after another, fondly recalling the early days she and Yehoshua had spent setting up their first home together. The linens, dishtowels, crystal-ware and even kitchen pots all evoked blissful newlywed memories as they found their way into the various closets of the new apartment.

It was shortly after four o'clock in the morning that the first hint of something not quite right was slowly realized.

"Do you perhaps have the box in there with the Shabbos flatware?" Devorah called out to Yehoshua from the kitchen. "I just found the perfect drawer to keep it in."

"Sorry Devorah, but I don't see any more kitchen boxes in here," he replied. "Maybe you came across it already and put it somewhere else by mistake?"

"No," said Devorah. "It's definitely not here. Do you maybe want to check again?"

Yehoshua briefly surveyed the remaining boxes in the salon but Yael's missing box didn't seem to be there.

"No, I'm afraid there's only seforim boxes left in here now. Nachman must have left it behind with the orbiter when he brought the rest over. I'll stop by him tomorrow and fetch it then. In the meantime, let's try and get some more sleep."

Yehoshua awoke rather late the next morning and it wasn't until lunchtime that he finally presented himself at the Hoffman apartment to reclaim his missing box. However, despite Yehoshua's insistence Nachman denied any knowledge of it.

"We made sure to bring all twenty seven boxes over," he explained, "and I even counted them twice to make sure we got them all."

"But that can't be," persisted Yehoshua. "We're still missing the box with the Shabbos flatware. Are you sure you still don't have it somewhere?"

"Positive! We made sure to clear out everything before your return. Twenty-seven boxes and the elliptical orbiter. There's nothing left here I assure you."

But this assurance only left Yehoshua even more confused.

"The *elliptical orbiter*? You returned that *also*?" he asked disbelievingly. "But that's not in the apartment *either*! I thought it was still by you and would let you keep it for a while more until we can get our lives back together."

"I......I don't know what to tell you," replied Nachman equally puzzled, "but it's not here anymore, that's for sure."

Dejected and empty-handed Yehoshua returned to his new apartment, not quite sure how to broach the subject of their missing possessions with Devorah. He needn't have bothered worrying. While he had been away Devorah had been making her own enquiries and had uncovered some ominous tidings regarding their new building.

"Yes, it was terrible what happened last week," confirmed Tzippy Braun. "Three apartments in the building were broken into and stolen from. I guess if you're missing one of your boxes then you must be number four."

"Oh no!" exclaimed Devorah. "That's terrible! Yehoshua will be so upset to hear."

As she had predicted, Yehoshua was more than a little challenged by the finality of her discovery, only adding to the misery by informing her of the apparent loss of the orbiter also.

"I just can't believe it!" he finally said in disbelief. "We don't even have insurance on the *dira* yet."

"Mrs. Braun said the police were working on the case but didn't hold out much hope for recovering any of the stolen goods," said Devorah, throwing up her arms in helpless resignation. "I guess there's nothing else we can really do about it then,"

"I suppose you're right," echoed an equally dejected Yehoshua. "Maybe we should just be grateful that they didn't take more stuff!"

Despite this mildly positive note, Yehoshua could not hide his distress at the loss, as his friend candidly pointed out the next day.

"Don't say you haven't managed to find that box yet?" Nachman asked. "I thought for sure it would have turned up by now."

In a tone full of melancholy Yehoshua explained to his friend about the series of break-ins in their building the previous week and how his missing box and the elliptical oribter had almost certainly been stolen.

"I feel terrible," said Nachman, genuinely disturbed by the news, "especially as it was partly my fault for bringing everything over to your house last week."

"Oh please, don't blame yourself!" chastised Yehoshua.

"No, I really mean it," countered Nachman. "Having your things stolen is just an awful thing to happen." He paused reflectively at this point for a few seconds before continuing. "But tell me, what was in that box anyway? My wife mentioned something about your Shabbos flatware, but there must have been more than just that in a box that size?"

This discomforting question saw Yehoshua lower his eyes to the ground in sobering contemplation as he shared with his friend the real magnitude of the loss.

"There *was* actually more than just the flatware in the box," he began painfully. "Do you remember two years ago when our flight here was diverted through Glasgow and they put us up in a hotel overnight?"

Nachman looked puzzled.

"Sure I remember it. But what's that got to do with the box?"

"The porter Nachman, the porter..." related Yehoshua as his friend's face slowly flushed with recognition. "Remember that very exclusive Scotch[1] he sold me. That was *also* in the box!"

Nachman gulped deeply at this painful declaration.

"Oh no!" he acknowledged, sadly. "I guess then I'll just have to pay you for that also," he said resignedly.

"Oh please, don't be ridiculous!" countered Yehoshua. "It's a shame about that scotch and the other stuff but it wasn't your fault that someone broke in and stole it."

---

1. see The Lost Scotch p. 29

"You don't understand!" countered Nachman. "Of course it was my fault! My wife even warned me before I brought round everything that it wasn't safe to leave them in an uninhabited *dira*. I told her not to be so paranoid but it seems she was right after all. Even if you don't want to let me pay she'll certainly make me!"

☞ *Does Nachman have to pay for the theft of the exercise orbiter and the missing box?* *(p. 247)*

Contents — בירורי הלכה

Preface

☞ *The Heavenly Tribunal seemed well pleased with Solly's decision not to evict the widow Bloch. Does that mean the Beis Din were wrong to rule in his favor?*

Not necessarily.

This would depend on the mandate the Beis Din received from the two litigants at the outset of the court case. While it is certainly preferable for a Beis Din to be granted superior powers of jurisdiction allowing them to consider the moral implications of a ruling, this is not mandatory. Should the litigants choose "straight Din", then moral considerations are set aside. A Beis Din will then be bound to follow the dictates of Halacha *only*, without regard to semantics.

The difficulty in a Beis Din ruling contrary to Halachic doctrine in favor of ethical concerns (without a special mandate) is that it essentially plays one-upmanship over G-d- while *His* Torah predicates one ruling, *this judge* would (humbly?) suggest ruling differently. In our situation, while our sympathies lie overwhelming in favor of the widow Bloch, the Halachic reality is that she is wrong and the Beis Din's decision then probably correct.

This axiom is surprisingly easy to grasp. An indigent widow often finds little Halachic sympathy when the kashrus of her family's weekly (weakly) chicken is questioned; a badly broken bone makes the fowl a *treifeh* irrespective of the financial worth of the questioner. A similar parallel exists in Choshen Mishpat. If money Halachically belongs to Reuven, no Dayan or Beis Din is authorized to rule in favor of his more financially challenged, debt-ridden, pitiable plaintiff, Shimon.

Nonetheless, all is not lost for where this Beis Din's mandate ends is where the individual's responsibility begins. Is it correct to blindly apply Halacha without due regard for extra-Halachic concerns? Would it be more sensible perhaps for a victor to grant a degree of leeway to the vanquished? These questions but scratch the surface of man's own obligation to seek spiritual and moral perfection within his own life. The Beis Din can declare what is the letter of the law but it is up to the individual to invoke its spirit.

With this in mind, one can better consider the significance of the following disclaimer.

This book is intended as a guide only. In cases of practical application a competent Rov should be consulted.

Getting the Halacha wrong is one problem. Sometimes however, even getting the Halacha right can be incorrect, the tale of Solly Weinreb being a most telling case in point.

1. The Wedding Drummer

☞ *Do Ari or his father have to pay for the damage done to Benny's drum set?*

Yes, or at least according to most authorities.

Although it is clear that Ari was responsible for breaking the drum set and would typically have to pay, an important technicality could exempt him. That technicality is termed shmira b'baalim, literally guardianship under employment[1] . When an employer borrows, rents or takes charge of an item belonging to his employee he does not have to pay for any loss or damage occurring to that item. Since Benny was working for Ari when Ari borrowed the drums, the dinim of shmira bbaalim would seemingly apply.

There is however a dispute amongst the authorities regarding the scope of this Bibilcal exemption. The majority opinion only extends it to include consequential damage which could have been averted by guarding the item better. However, where the damage was caused directly by the employer himself, as in our case, the exemption would not apply.

---

1. The source for this law is Scriptural. The relevant verses appear in Exodus ch. 22 vs. 13-14.

'וכי ישאל איש מעם רעהו ונשבר או מת בעליו אין עמו לא ישלם. אם בעליו עמו לא ישלם וכו'

"If a person borrows from his friend and the item subsequently dies or breaks, the borrower pays only if the owner is not in his employ. If however he is working for him then there is no payment."

Nonetheless, there is a significant minority opinion that do apply the *shmira bbaalim* exception to damage even caused directly, which does give some leeway to exempt Ari.

It should also be noted that the exemption is only relevant if it was Ari himself who hired (and paid for) the drummer. Only the actual employer has the exemption and if it was really Ari's father who was the big boss then Ari would certainly have to pay for the damage he caused.

איתא במחבר סי' שמו סע' א וז"ל השואל והיה המשאיל עם השואל במלאכתו בשעה שמשך הדבר השאול אפי' נגנב או נאבד בפשיעה פטור שנאמר אם בעליו עמו לא ישלם עכ"ל.

ועי' בפתחי תשובה סי' קעו ס"ק יג וז"ל גם במל"מ פ"ה מהל' שותפין דעתו כן דכל המשנה מדעת שותפו שעשה מעשה בידים והפסיד חייב אף היכי דהוה שמירה בבעלים דלא אמרינן פשיעה בבעלים פטור אלא היכי דהיה היזק ע"י שנתרשל שלא שמר יפה אבל אם עשה מעשה והפסידו בידים הוי מזיק גמור וחייב אף בבעלים וכתב דלכאורה תליא במחלוקת הרמב"ם והראב"ד פ"ט מהלכות אישות דין ט באשה ששברה כלים בעת שעשתה מלאכתה בתוך ביתה שכתב הרמב"ם דפטורה לא מן הדין אלא תקנה משום שלום בית והראב"ד שם השיג דמן הדין נמי פטורה שהיא פשיעה בבעלים דכל שעה שכיר לה משמע דס"ל להראב"ד דאין חילוק בין פשיעה למזיק בידים גם הה"מ שדחה דברי הראב"ד מטעם דאין שכיר לה אלא בשעה שנתעסק בצרכיה משמע דמודה נמי להראב"ד. אך באמת י"ל דגם הראב"ד מודה וכו' מ"מ אחרי שדעת הראב"ד והה"מ דכל עניני שוגג המזיקים בידים מיפטרו מטעם שמירה בבעלים אפשר דהמוחזק יכול לומר קים לי כוותייהו ע"ש היטב עכ"ל.

וע"ע בחכמת שלמה סימן תכא סעי' ג וז"ל דאדם מועד לעולם בין שוגג בין מזיד בין ער בין ישן וכו' עיין במשל"מ וכו' מה שרוצה לחלק בדעת הראב"ד פכ"א מהל' אישות דס"ל דלענין שמירה בבעלים הוי רק דין אדם מועד לעולם

רק בדין פושע ופטור בבעלים בלא נתכוין להזיק ועיין בחיבורי לאהע"ז מה' ה סימן יז מ"ש בזה לק"ק אוסטרהא לחלק בין שומר לאדם דדוקא בשומר פטור בין מזיק בבעלים ולא בשאר עיי"ש.

ונ"ל לציין עוד כאן דברי הרמ"א סי' שעח סעי' ט וז"ל בחורים הרוכבים לקראת חתן וכלה והזיקו זה את זה ממון דרך שמחה ושחוק וכן בשאר דבר שמחה הואיל ונהגו כן פטורים עכ"ל וע"ע בש"ך סי' שמ ס"ק ה אם יש שם סניף להקל על החתן ודו"ק.

2. Es-rogue

☞ *Would Mr. Berman be entitled to a refund from Jake for the extra hundred dollars he was charged?*

☞ *Was Meir allowed to divulge to Mr. Berman that he was offered that same esrog for one hundred dollars less than Mr. Berman paid?*

1. No.

This question bases itself around the Halachos of *oyna'ah,* overcharging. Typically, if someone unknowingly pays or charges in excess of one sixth above or below market price for an item, the sale of that item is invalid. However, in certain specialty markets these Halachos are suspended. This is because the nature of the market is not given over to the critical analysis necessary to accurately evaluate the true market price of the item to determine when the sixth threshold is reached.

One of the exceptions highlighted in Halachic responsa is the *esrog* market. Since the market is extremely volatile with prices constantly fluctuating the laws of *oyna'ah* are suspended and a seller may not have to issue a refund.

Nonetheless, it should be noted that this is only after the sale has taken place. For a seller to alter his prices based on how much he feels he can extract from a worthy customer is unscrupulous, and setting out to act in such a way is certainly wrong and incorrect.

2. Once we have ascertained this we can answer the second question in the negative also.

The *Chofetz Chaim* points out that these two *Halachos* are very much dependent upon each other. The only leniency to inform a previous customer of a seller's treacherous pricing policies is when the customer would be entitled to a refund. Since in our case Jake would probably not grant Mr. Berman a refund there would be no purpose in speaking ill of him for no good reason.

Nonetheless, one would be permitted to warn Jake's potential customers in future years of his suspicious pricing strategies. This would be an appropriate preventative measure to prevent him from profiting unethically in the future.

איתא במחבר סי' רכז סעי' א אסור להונות את חבירו בין במקחו בין בממכרו ואיזה מהם שאינה בין לוקח בין מוכר עובר בלאו ובסעי' ב' כמה תהיה אונאה ויהיה חייב להשיב שתות בשוה כיצד הרי שמכר שוה שש בחמש או שוה שבע בשש או שוה חמש בשש או שוה שש בשבע ה"ז אונאה.

ויש לעיין בתשובת בית יצחק או"ח סי' קח שהביא שיטת הבית יוסף ריש סי' רט וז"ל הנה בריטב"א קדושין ח' כ' דהיכא דמוכר חפץ לחבירו בשיתא ובשוק לא שוה אלא ה' אי להאי לוקח שוה אין בו משום אונאה וכו' הנה מתחילת דברי הריטב"א י"ל לכאורה בקונה אתרוג לצרכו אף דכשישאל לתגר יאמר ששוה פחות מ"מ אין בו אונאה דהמוכר יכול לטעון דלדידך שוה יותר כיון שבאתרוגים תליא השיווי לפי האדם אך זה אינו דדוקא כשנודע בבירור דלדידי' שוה יותר אין בו אונאה וכו' אבל בסתמא ל"ק רק כפי מה ששוה ול"מ המוכר לומר לדידך שוה יותר וז"פ.

ולכאורה י"ל כיון דפסקינן דיש אונאה לספרים ה"ה באתרוג ושוב ראיתי במח"א דיני אונאה סי' כד דמייתי לב"י סי' רא בדבר שאין שער ידוע כמו

גיזה וחלב אין בו אונאה ומח"א הקשה מספרים די"ב אונאה וצ"ל דס"ל להב"י דספרים יש בו שומא ידוע ואמנם בזה אין הלכה כהב"י כמבואר בש"ך סי' רט ס"ק א. אמנם מייתי שם תשובת הרא"ש כלל י"ג סי' כ' שכ' דל"ש אונאה אלא בחפץ שדמי' ידועים ונתאנה בשומת החפץ וכו' ומזה משמע קצת כדברי הב"י על כן נלפע"ד דבאתרוג כיון דהשער משתנה בכל שעה גם הש"ך מודה ועכ"פ המוכר יכול לומר קים לי כהב"י וא"ב דין אונאה אם לא שבקי אומר שהאתרוג פסול עכ"ל.

ועי' בספר חפץ חיים הלכות רכילות כלל ט הלכה יא וז"ל וכל זה אם הוא רוצה להזהירו כדי שלא יבוא לידי אונאה אבל אם כבר לקח מאחד סחורה והוא יודע שרמהו או בשיווי המקח או בשאר חסרונות תלוי בזה: אם על פי דין תורה אין לו עתה על המתאנה כלום בין מפני שהאונאה בשיווי המקח היתה בפחות משתות ובין מפני שעבר הזמן כדי שיראה לתגר או לקרובו או שאר סבה שבגללה הפסיד המתאנה בודאי מי שהולך ומעורר להמתאנה ומראהו איך שפלוני רמהו עובר על איסור רכילות כיון דעל פי דין תורה אין לו עליו עתה כלום שוב לא הוי הסיפור כי אם דברים בעלמא והוא כרוכל שנזכר בכל מקום שהוא טוען דברים מזה לזה ואפילו אם המתאנה שואלו גם כן לא יאמר לו האמת עכ"ל.

3. Uzi goes to court

☞ *Would Chaim have fared better in the Din Torah had he not agreed to pshoro-compromise and insisted on strict Din instead?*

No. He probably would have done worse.

Of the two main claims against Uzi, neither have any real *Halachic* validity.

The two thousand dollar a month late penalty clause presents a problem of *asmachta*-gambling and would not be valid.

When Uzi quoted the price for the work he was obviously confident he would be able to complete the job within the prescribed time frame and had no intention to watch his profits disappear due to unforeseen and unavoidable circumstances. Without the correct structuring necessary to avoid this *asmachta* problem, the penalty clause would be invalid.

The elevation in Uzi's price is also in order, especially as the original figure given was only intended as an estimate. If a worker quotes for a job and it transpires that more work was required than had first been thought or that price fluctuations increase the cost AND the worker was not being irresponsible or untruthful when he had provided the first quote, he is entitled to charge the customer the higher price to reflect the work actually done.

Obviously this is not a license for abuse. On the contrary, if a worker knowingly quotes below what he knows it will cost to complete the job he has consciously and deliberately foregone charging more than the quoted figure. Our *Halacha* only applies when a genuine error had occurred.

Mr. Bennaroch's grievance for the cost of relocating his daughter's day camp is also without *Halachic* merit. Since Uzi had not been made aware beforehand that the day camp was contingent upon his expedience he never knowingly accepted any financial responsibility for the expense. In fact, it was only because a *pshoro* was agreed upon that The Benarroches received any compensation from the Beis Din at all. The five hundred dollars was awarded because of the day camp cost, which the *Dayonim* felt was not an unjust penalty for Uzi to agree to, given the leeway allowed under the *pshoro* banner.

Contrary to popular belief, a *pshoro* is not an automatic withdrawal of rights or foregoing of monies. Even when one has agreed to a *pshoro* he may still be awarded payment in full if the opposing party has no valid or legitimate claim to suggest otherwise. Only in situations when key facts may be unclear, when a Halachic impasse occurs between the authorities, or sometimes for the sake of maintaining peace between warring factions will the leeway allotted to the Dayonim under the banner of *pshoro* be invoked.

Further, an uncooperative debtor whose sole motivation in submitting to a Beis Din is to save money through a *pshoro*-compromise settlement is contravening *Halacha*. In such a case, any negotiated discount is invalid and the debtor obligated to pay in full.

☞ *The Pele Yoetz advises one who plans on doing home construction to budget for double of what he thinks it will cost.*

ଔ ଔ ଔ

טענתו הראשון דאיתא בהחוזה שביניהם קנסות עבור האיחור לכאו' אין לחייבו דהנם בגדר אסמכתא ולא היה בידו לזרז פועליו יותר ממה שעשה וכמו דאיתא בסי' רז סעי' יג ברמ"א וז"ל ויש אומרים דג' חילוקים בדיני אסמכתא דכל מה שאין בידו ותלוי ביד אחרים כגון שא"ל קנה לי יין ממקום פלוני ואם לא תקנה תחייב לי בכך וכך דזה אינו תלוי בו דדילמא לא ירצו למכור לו אסמכתא בכל ענין ולא קנה עכ"ל.

וע"ע שם סעי' טז לענין קנסות בסתם ואביא דברי המחבר בקיצור וז"ל קנס שעושים בשידוכים לקנוס החוזר בו לא הוי אסמכתא כי כדאי הוא שיתחייב החוזר בו בקנס לדמי הבושת שבייש את חבירו וכן אם המלמד קבל עליו בעת שהשכירוהו קנס אם יחזור בו ולא נמצא מלמד אחר מזומן אינו אסמכתא עכ"ל ועי' בסמ"ע ס"ק מח וז"ל ולא נמצא מלמד כו' דג"כ מפסיד הבע"ה שיהיה בנו בטל ופסידא דלא הדר הוא עכ"ל ומבואר דדוקא במאורעות מיוחדין מועילין קנסות אבל כשאין ההפסד אלא איחור וטירחא לכאו' יש בקנס חסרון של אסמכתא כ"נ.

טענתו השני' במה שהגביה המחיר יותר ממה שאומר לו הקבלן לכתחילה אפילו נניח שהמשכיר מגלה דעתו שאינו רוצה לשלם יותר מסכום הנזכר מ"מ מאחר שבאמת הנאתו יותר מזה הסכום ק' מאד לומר שהקבלן אחראי על העילוי דמים וכעין מה דאיתא בסי' שלב סעי' א וז"ל אמר לשלוחו צא ושכור לי פועלים בשלשה והלך ושכרן בארבעה וכו' ואם אמר להם שכרכם על בעל הבית נותן להם בעל הבית כמנהג המדינה עכ"ל ועי' בספר מעיני החכמה ב"מ פ"ו עו' א' ד"ה ברש"י וליחזי וז"ל לכאורה הוא נגד שכל אחר שפירש בעה"ב שאינו רוצה ליתן רק תלתא אפילו נשכרים כולם בארבעה מ"מ הוא לא רצה ליתן רק תלתא ואטו אם יאמר בעה"ב בתלתא והפועל יודע שהפועלים נשכרים בארבעה יעבוד עבודתו וע"כ יתן לו ארבע זו דבר שאין הדעת מחייבו וכבר עלה בדעתי דכאן הקושיא כיון שעינינו רואות שהמלאכה שוה ארבעה א"כ יוכלו הפועלים לומר שאין מאמינין לבע"ה שאמר לו בתלתא ומחוייב ליתן להם ארבע

מאחר שידוע שפעולה זו נשכרת בארבע וכו' דמסתמא לא התנה לשנות ממנהג הפועלים וכו' . עוד ממה שאמר בע"ה לתלתא אין ראיה לומר שהוא דוקא כיון שכולם נשכרין בארבע יש לנו לומר שבעה"ה כיון שהוא צריך לפועלים א"כ מסתמא לא עלה בדעתו שאם לא ימצא בתלתא שלא לשכור פועלים כלל לכן יש לנו לומר שלא אמר בע"ה דוקא בתלתא רק אם ימצא כן אבל אם כולם נשכרים בארבע יש לנו לומר שאינו קפידא דוקא בתלתא ואי קפיד דוקא על תלתא הו"ל לאתנויי שלא יתן יותר בפירוש וכו' עכ"ל.

ועי' בשו"ע סי' יב בפ"ת ס"ק ג וז"ל סתם פשר הוא מלשון פושרין לא קר ולא חם וכדאמרי' (בב"ב דף קל"ג ע"ב) דייני חצצתא פרש"י דייני פשרה שחולקין הדבר והוא מלשון מחצה כן הוא ע"פ רוב אלא דמ"מ יש רשות ביד הפשרן לעשות לפי מהות הדבר לפי ראות עיניו לעשות שלום בין הצדדים בלי נטיית צד ובנדון ...שקיבל לעשות פשר קרוב לדין נ"ל דפחות שליש מקרי קרוב לדין דהיינו אם חייב ע"פ הדין שלש מאות יפשר בשני מאות שליש פחות וזה מקרי קרוב וכו' אך על כל פנים לא יהיה זה שיעור מוחלט שלא לפחות מזה ואם יראה בעיניו שבדבר מועט יכול לפשר בעל דינו בענין שיהא שלום ביניהם ודאי טפי עדיף כיון שע"פ הדין זוכה לגמרי כלל הדבר הכל תלוי בראות עיני הפשרן ועכ"פ לא יותר משליש שחייב או פטור ע"פ הדין כי פחות משני שלישים מקרי רחוק ע"ש עכ"ל.

וע"ע בסי' יב סעי' ו וז"ל מי שתובעים אותו ממון שהוא מוחזק בו אסור לבקש צדדים להשמט כדי שיתרצה הלה לעשות עמו פשרה וימחול לו על השאר. הגה ואם עבר ועשה אינו יוצא ידי שמים עד שיתן לו את שלו עכ"ל.

ואלו הן דברי הפלא יועץ ענין בנין וז"ל אמרו רבותינו ז"ל : כל העוסק בבנין מתמסכן (סוטה יא.) רחמנא ליצלן שבכל ההוצאות אדם יודע לחשב כמה יוציא ומסתכל בכיסו אם יוכל להוציא מוציא באפן שלא יבוא להתמסכן לא כן העוסק בבנין שחושב להוציא מאה ונעשה לו הוצאה ממאתים ומשהתחיל אינו יכול למשוך ידו ומתוך כך יכול לבוא להתמסכן ולכן ראוי לגבר שיחשוב תחלה אם יכול להוציא כפלים על אשר אמדו שצריך לאותו הבנין יתעסק בבנין ואם לא לא יתעסק שצריך לראות על החנות תחלה כדאמרי אינשי החנות בונה הבית ואין הבית בונה החנות עכ"ל.

4. Impounded

☞ *Is Moshe Dovid responsible for the police impounding fees?*

Yes.

Once he had taken charge of the car it remained his responsibility until it was returned according to the original agreement. That agreement stipulated that it had to be parked in the car's correct spot outside the Silver's home. Since it was not, but instead one space over, it was not considered returned and hence remained Moshe Dovid's responsibility. When the police came and 'stole' it, Moshe Dovid remained liable for the theft.

Nonetheless, certain mitigating factors may exist which could give room for some leniency; ultimately the car remained intact, undamaged and easily retrievable by its owner. Any fees the police may be charging are only indirect and according to some opinions not the responsibility of the guardian.

ᏣᏒ ᏣᏒ ᏣᏒ

איתא במחבר סי' שז סעי' א וז"ל השוכר מחבירו בהמה או כלים דינו כשומר שכר להתחייב בגניבה ואבידה וליפטר מאונסין עכ"ל וכיון שחייב גם על גניבה ואבידה ממילא אין צריך לדון כלל אם מה שהניח המכונית חשוב כפשיעה או לא דאפילו נניח שאינו פשיעה מ"מ חיובי השוכר כולל גניבה ג"כ.

ויש לעיין בספר דברי חיים חלק חו"מ הלכות שומרים סי' יד וז"ל והנה כשנגנב בפשיעה ונמצא הגנב הי' נראה לכאורה דלכ"ע מחוייב השומר לשלם לבעלים דהא כיון שפשע נתחייב והשומר ידון עם הגנב ובהא אף שהשומר לא יוכל אח"כ להוציא מהגנב השומר מחוייב לשלם להבעלים כדין שומר שפשע אך יש לעיין מהא דמבואר ברשב"א בב"ק (דף קח) וכו' דהרשב"א סובר אף דשומר חייב בפשיעה היינו בנאבד הפקדון ואינו בעולם אבל בנמצא הגנב ויכולין הבעלים להוציא מיד הגנב את הפקדון אין השומר מחוייב לשלם דיכול לומר לא הפסדתי אותך והרי שלך לפניך כי תוכל לילך אל הגנב וכו' ואם הפקדון תו אינו בעין ביד הגנב בהא י"ל דחייב השומר לשלם לבעלים כדין שומר שפשע והוא ידון עם הגנב עכ"ל.

אבל מדבריו אינו מבורר אם השומר חייב בהוצאות שצריך לשלם כדי שיחזיר הגנב החפץ להבעלים. וזה דומה למה דאיתא בב"ק צח. הזורק מטבע של חבירו לים הגדול פטור מ"ט הא אמר הא מנח קמך אי בעית שקליה (רש"י- הא מנח קמך ואינה אבודה ואי משום דבעי למיתב זוזא לבר אמוראה למישט ולמישקליה גרמא הוא שגורם להפסידו אותו שכר וגרמא בניזקין פטור) והני מילי דאדיי' אדווי אבל שקליה בידיה מיגזל גזליה השבה בעי מיעבד עכ"ל ומבואר מזה דאינו חייב על הוצאות בר אמוראה להוציא החפץ ממים צלולין אלא אם נתחייב בהשבת החפץ. ולזה יש לעיין בדברי הנתיה"מ סי' פו ס"ק א וז"ל בס' קצוה"ח כ' דבפקדון לא שייך שעבודא דר' נתן דאפילו חיוב חזרה לא מתחיל עד שעת פשיעה וכו' ע"ש והא ודאי ליתא כמו שמבואר בסי' נח בש"ך ס"ק ט וז"ל שם כיון שבא לידו בתורת פקדון דצריך לעשות השבה גמורה כו' עכ"ל ומה שמביא ראיה מהא דכתובות מהיתה לו פרה שאולה וטבחה בשבת לאו ראיה היא דשם דנין על חיוב תשלומין שנתחייב על הטביחה לשלם מן העליה דזה ודאי לא יתחיל עד שעת הטביחה דחיוב חזרה אינו אלא כשהפקדון עדיין בעין אבל כשאינו בעין פקע חיוב חזרה ומתחיל חיוב התשלומין וכו' אבל כשהוא בעין יש חיוב הגוף על החזרה ולא שיעבוד נכסי עכ"ל.

וע"ע בתשובות חקרי לב חו"מ סי' מ וז"ל עמדתי לברר דין זה במעשה שהיה בראובן שהיה לו כלי יין דהיינו חביות גדולות ולפי שלא מצא מי שיקנה אותם נתנם בשאלה לשמעון ונשרפו בשריפה שנשרף ביתו אם חייב שמעון לשלם לראובן שויים ככל שואל דחייב באונסין שי"ל דבכהאי גוונא פטור שהרי היה לו למשאיל הנאה שאם היו נשארות בידו שנה אחת ריקנות היו מתקלקלות וגם לא היה בידו להשכירם כיון דהשואל הנזכר קנה הגאבילה של יין ולפי תקנת העיר אין רשות לאחר להניח יין וגם שאם היו נשארים בידו היה צריך לשכור

מקום בשכירות כדי להניחם שם וא"כ כיון שיש לו הנאה למשאיל ג"כ הו"ל נהנה ומהנה דהוי שומר שכר דאינו חייב באונסין ודמי למ"ש בב"מ (פא.א) השאלני והשאלך דהוי שומר שכר. אך אחר הישוב הא לא איריא שהרי בב"מ (צד.ב) גבי מ"ש שואל כל הנאה שלו הקשו וכו' ע"ש שהאריך בראיות וכ' בסוף התשובה ברור בנדון דידן דשואל גמור הוי וחייב באונסין עכ"ל.

5. Squirrels

☞ *Is Norman entitled to a refund from Rafi for not doing his job properly?*

Yes.

Rafi knew that Norman was only having his roof fixed to solve the squirrel problem and also knew that he only agreed to have the work done because of Rafi's assurance that it would indeed solve the problem. In providing that assurance recklessly Rafi assumed responsibility that his work would solve the squirrel problem. Since it didn't, he has to reimburse Norman for wasting three hundred dollars on a needless repair.

It is important to appreciate here the subtle difference between amateur and professional advice. Professional advice can only come from a professional- one whose experience and knowledge give him a thorough understanding of the subject matter at hand. When advice is dispensed against such a backdrop it can be presumed to have considered any likely consequence, hence anything untoward occurring subsequently would be considered as have been unforeseeable and sufficient reason to absolve the professional from guilt and obligation.

Not so with amateur advice. Not possessing a thorough knowledge of the issues at hand, the amateur is irresponsible for offering an opinion at the outset and as a result carries financial responsibility for losses occurring as a result of that advice being taken[2].

ଓ ଓ ଓ

איתא במחבר סי' שו סעי' ו, המראה דינר לשולחני ואמר לו יפה הוא ונמצא רע אם בשכר ראהו חייב לשלם אע"פ שהוא בקי ואינו צריך להתלמד ואם בחנם ראהו פטור והוא שיהיה בקי שאינו צריך להתלמד ואם אינו בקי חייב לשלם אע"פ שהוא בחנם והוא שיאמר לשולחני עליך אני סומך או שהיו הדברים מראים שהוא סומך על ראייתו ולא יראה לאחרים.

ועוד, שם בסעי' ז' טבח שעושה בחנם וניבל וכן שולחני שאמר יפה ונמצא רע וכן כל כיוצא בזה עליהם להביא ראיה שהם מומחין ואם לא הביאו ראי' משלמין עכ"ל.

ונראה מזה דטענת ראובן באמת מחייבו ולא פטרו, דאם היה מומחה יכול לטעון דאונס הוי מה שחזרו לו השרצים אבל מאחר שאינו מומחה אין לו לומר דיעה על דבר שאינו בקי בו כשיודע שהבעה"ב סומך עליו.

---

2 See also SHATNEZ!, book one p.214

6. Fate and Fortune

☞ *Is Reuven entitled to recover all, or even part of the half million dollars Shimon and Shiri received from their father's life insurance policy?*

No. However he may be entitled to recover half of the premium paid to maintain the policy.

The insurance company paid according to the terms of a policy which provided for half a million dollars to each child. This was the policy for which Reuven paid the premium- there was no policy paying Reuven alone; therefore his assiduousness will not affect the payout.

Even recovering a mere half of the premium is also not straightforward. The *Halacha* highlights the case of two captives trapped in prison and one hired the services of a lawyer to plead on his behalf. The courts heard the petition and released both prisoners as a result. The prisoner who hired the lawyer is not entitled to charge his compatriot for the legal services. Since he had to pay the lawyer anyway and would have paid the same even with the absence of a second captive, it is of poor character to deny the other prisoner the 'free ride'. This is categorized by the *Halacha* as being *middas S'dom*- a trait of the Sodomites.

In our story, since Reuven needed to pay the full premium just to recover his own half million without paying any extra for his sister's share it could be *middas S'dom* to subsequently charge his sister for the premium.

However, there is a significant difference. While it was necessary to pay the full premium to reap the benefit of just the half million, nonetheless the effort was towards a full million dollar payout, albeit to two individuals. There was no single effort for one half a million which just so happened to generate a second half million payout. This differs from the prisoners' case where the lawyer's efforts were specifically for only one of the prisoners.

ঔ ঔ ঔ

איתא ברמ"א סי' רסד סעי' ד וז"ל שנים שנתפסו והוציא אחד הוצאות אם השני יצא מן המאסר בלא השתדלות חבירו אין חייב ליתן לחבירו כלום הואיל ולא התנה עמו ואם לא יצא רק על ידי השתדלות האחר לא יוכל לומר לא הייתי צריך להשתדלותך כי ידי תקיפה אע"פ שהאמת אתו מ"מ חייב ליתן לו כפי מה שנהנה לפי ראות ב"ד כן נ"ל ואם נראה לב"ד שלא הוצרך להרבות בהוצאות בשבילו דאפי' בשבילו לבדו היה צריך לכל הוצאות אלו אינו חייב ליתן לו כלום דזה נהנה וזה אינו חסר עכ"ל וממילא בנ"ד הספק מבואר דכיון דאי אפשר לראובן להרויח מהאינשוראנס בלי תשלום כל ההוצאות ממילא הנאת אחיו הוי בכלל זה נהנה וזה לא חסר הואיל ולא התנה עמו לשלם מתחלה.

ויש לעיין בנתיה"מ שם ס"ק ו וז"ל סיים הרמ"א דאם ירד על דעת שניהם דחייב ליתן לו והטעם נראה כיון דא"א להציל בלי הוצאות ממילא כ"א יכול לכוף את חבירו ליתן וכו' שכן הדין בכל מקום כשהדבר צריך לשנחהם וא"א לאחד לתקן הדבר מבלי חבירו שכופין זה את זה עכ"ל.

וע"ע בדבריו סי' קע"ח ס"ק ג וז"ל אפילו בשנים שאינם שותפין כל שיש דבר שהוא מוכרח לשניהן ואין אחד רוצה לעשותן יכול השני לכפותו עכ"ל.. אבל עם כל זה יש לדחות מאחר שאין מיתת הנפטר מוכרח ויכול לטעון שמעון שאין הדבר עומד להשתלם וממילא א"א להכריחו לשלם.

7. A Car and its Owner

☞ *Who does the insurance money really belong to?*

The insurance money belongs to whoever owns the car.

However, the question of who owns the car is far from straightforward. Therefore it would seem appropriate that Chaim reimburse the Senderowitzs for the street value of the car, keeping the insurance excess for himself.

One needs to consider here two distinct values associated with the car. One is the value of the physical entity- how much the vehicle is worth as a mode of transportation or status symbol. The second is more abstract- how much the vehicle is worth as a speculative investment for generating other funds merely by dint of its existence, similar perhaps to the value associated with a lottery ticket.

The value of the car's physical entity certainly belonged to the Senderowitzs from the moment they took possession of it. However, prior to filing for title of the car it is difficult to say they had taken ownership of the speculative value of the automobile also. Even if we presume that Chaim had already given it away, without the Senderowitzs having registered the title in their name any *profits* gained from the car remain essentially ownerless or *hefker*. Chaim, being the original owner and recipient of the check would then have acquired the insurance check at least from this vacuum perspective. Therefore to remove the entire check from Chaim seems *Halachically* incorrect. Additionally, the elevated payment above the actual physical value of the car was a product of the insurance industry's own ordinances, part of which system recognizes solely the registered owner as the true owner of the vehicle.

In reality one could even question the obligation to pay the Senderowitzs four hundred dollars. The insurance company sent Chaim the check because as far as they were concerned he was the owner of the vehicle. Even if they were mistaken and should have sent part or all of the money to Sender, the fact that they didn't is not necessarily Chaim's responsibility. On the contrary, Mr. Stubbs is the one who should remain ultimately responsible for compensating Sender for the loss since he was the one who caused the damage. The fact that his insurance company failed in their responsibility is nothing to do with the Senderowitzs.

☙ ☙ ☙

איתא בסי׳ שז סעי׳ ה השוכר פרה מחבירו והשאילה לאחר ומתה כדרכה או נאנסה כיון שהשני חייב תחזור לבעלים הראשונים שאין הלה עושה סחורה בפרתו של חבירו ע״כ והענין בזה דאע״פ שמעקרא דדינא חייב השואל למשאיל שלו עבור האונס ומשאיל זה פטור מלשלם זה הממון למשכיר שלו מפני שהוא פטור מאונסין מ״מ קבעו חז״ל שאין אדם יכול לעשות סחורה בפרתו של אחר וממילא א״א להניח המעות אצל השוכר שאין הפרה שלו. וה״ה בנדונינו דאליבא דהלכתא אחר המשיכה כבר נקנה המכונית להמקבל לגמרי וא״כ האיך יכול הנותן להרויח בפרה שאינו שלו.

אלא שיש לדחות דבשלמא בשוכר שמתחלה כל הפרה קנוי להבעלים והשוכר לא קנה ממנו אלא שכירות שהוא זכות השתמשות בעלמא לכן כשנאבדה הפרה מן העולם אין לו שום זכויות כלפי היזקות ואבידת הפרה דכל קניני השוכר אינו אלא עבור פירות הפרה ולא בגופה וריוח זה בא מגוף הפרה ולא ממעשיה. וכיון שאין לו בהפרה כלום ממילא נקראת פרתו של אחר ואין

לו להרויח בה. אבל בנדונינו מעולם לא זכה המקבל לגבות הביטוח כלל כל זמן שלא נרשמה המכונית על שמו אצל הממשלה. וא"כ זכות זה עדיין אצל הנותן הוא ואינו נקרא פרתו של חבירו דהרי ההנאה זו לא באה מעצם גוף המכונית ורק זה הגוף ניתן להמקבל. ויותר מזה שאפילו קודם התאונה לא היתה המכונית שוה אלא כארבע מאה דולר ואין חברת ביטוח משלמין יותר רק משום שכן הם חוקי המדינה . אשר על כן אין להמקבל תביעה אלא משום דינא דמלכותא ונמצא קרח מכאן ומכאן, דהלא כפי חוקי המדינה אין במשיכתו שום קנין כל זמן שלא נרשם כן אצל הממשלה.

ונראה עוד דיש לדמות זה למה דאיתא במחבר סי' קצד סעי' ב ישראל שלקח שדה מהעכו"ם ונתן דמים וקודם שיחזיק בה בא ישראל אחר והחזיק בה כדרך שמחזיקים בנכסי הגר זכה אחרון וכו' מפני שהעכו"ם מעת שלקח הדמים סילק רשותו וישראל לא קנה עד שיגיע השטר לידו ונמצאו נכסים אלו כנכסי מדבר וכו' והנה בנידונינו אע"פ שהנותן נסתלק במשיכת המקבל מ"מ אין המקבל זוכה כלפי הממשלה עד שנרשם אצליהם וא"כ בינתים זכות זה הוא כנכסי מדבר והפקר ויכול הנותן לזכות בו אם האינטשורנס שלחוה לו. והגם שהמחבר מסיק שם שהראשון חייב להחזיר לשני מעותיו, לכאורה בנדונינו סגי בחזרת מעות שויות המכונית והיתרון ששילמו חברת הביטוח יכול לזכות בו הנותן.

8. Tutor Troubl e

☞ *Is Ashira entitled to the full sixty dollars for her services, as her investigation suggests is the going rate?*

No.

While it may be true that Ashira's enquiries led *her* to establish a rate of sixty dollars per lesson, Mrs. Neumann's enquiries cannot be discounted either. The true going rate is established by considering *all* the quoted rates in the marketplace and then calculating what the midpoint is. This figure becomes the default going rate, which is what was agreed upon at the outset. In our case, this would be forty five dollars a lesson.

Ashira's claim that she provided a warm, loving environment which helped encourage young Dina's performance may well be true, but would not be considered reason for an elevated wage. On the contrary, any tutor is expected to provide an environment conducive to successful study as a basic requirement. Allowing Ashira to charge extra for providing such a service, would, by default establish a lower rate for tutors *failing* to provide such a situation. They would be better simply removed from service.

איתא במחבר סי' שלא סעי' ג השוכר את הפועל ואמרו לו כאחד וכשנים מבני העיר מחשבין היתר שבשכירות והפחות שבשכירות ומה שביניהם נותן החצי כגון אם היתר בשש והפחות בארבע נותן להם חמש.

9. Destination Beijing

☞ *Is Jeremy allowed to submit the false invoice and claim his full allowance for the trip?*

No.

An expense account pays for expenses. This was not an expense.

Although Jeremy was authorized to spend the full amount, he didn't and hence cannot charge the company for something he was not out of pocket from.

This *Halacha* should not be confused with a similar case where an employee receives something *extra* during a transaction. In such circumstance the employee *does* have some rights regarding the extra windfall. (see Cheesecake p. 238)

ᘓ ᘓ ᘓ

איתא בש"ך סי' קפג ס"ק יז וז"ל ראובן ששלח עם משכנות שלו להלוות לו עליהם מעכו"ם כפי שיוכל להמציא מהם והשליח אומר שהמציא בסך כך וכך וראובן נודע לו אח"כ שלוה בפחות מסך שאמר אין לראובן ליתן כ"א מה שנותן השליח לעכו"ם וכו' והוא פשוט בעיני ונכון עכ"ל.

וע"ע בבאר הגולה אות צ שנותן טעם לדבר וז"ל והיינו משום דהמעות של המשלח והנשאר ברשות דמרא קיימא עכ"ל.

10. The Rosh Yeshiva's Matzos

☞ *What is the Halacha the Rosh Yeshiva was referring to?*

"When an emissary accepts separate errands from two individuals but mixes their monies together such that they become indiscernible one from the other, the two become partners, each owning an equal share in any purchase."

When Heshy received the money from his friends he did not differentiate between the actual paper bills given and simply mixed them up. This inadvertent action created an even partnership between Duvy and Leiby, which even Heshy is not authorized to favor one friend over the other.

ꟹ ꟹ ꟹ

איתא במחבר סי' קפד סעי' א ג' שנתנו מעות לאחד לקנות להם מקח אם היו המעות מעורבים וקנה במקצת דמים אע"פ שהיתה כוונת השליח שזה שקנה לא' מהם הרי המקח של כולם וחולקים אותו לפי מעותיהן. היו מעות של כל א' מהם צרורים וחתומים אע"פ שהיה בלב השליח הזה שקנה המקח לכלם לא קנה אלא זה שקנה המקח במעותיו בלבד.

11. Catered Caper

☞ *Does Yoel have to pay for the cold catering?*

No.

Since Yoel ordered a full catering service the food remained the responsibility of the caterer until it was actually served. Therefore, even though the electrical malfunction was not at all the caterer's fault nonetheless it was his food and not Yoel's that got ruined. Without food, Ovadia was unable to do his job therefore has no valid claim against Yoel for payment.

A secondary question is whether Yoel owes the caterer for destroying the food that prevented him from doing his job in the first place. However, given the facts that the caterer knew the hotplate was borrowed, that Yoel had no idea whether it worked or not and that the damage done to the other hotplates was certainly indirect, Yoel could not be made to pay. Additionally, arriving so late at the hall on Friday precluded Ovadia from making a necessary check later, further reason to exonerate Yoel.

The owner of the actual hotplate would also not be liable. Ultimately, the soup, which was on his hotplate, *was* served and the damage caused to the other hotplates is too indirect and unintentional to obligate him.

☞ *A happy ending: Yoel paid the caterer in full anyway. The caterer had not profited from the mishap and had still incurred the expenses of purchasing and preparing all of the food. Yoel had already budgeted for the caterer's entire fee and felt it unfair to profit from the hapless caterer's unfortunate loss, his own disappointment notwithstanding.*

ଔ ଔ ଔ

איתא בסי׳ שיא סעי׳ ה שכר ספינה סתם ליין סתם הרי אלו חולקין השכר ודוקא כשאין אחד מהם רוצה להשלים אבל זה מביא יינו וזה אינו מביא ספינה אם נתן שכר נמי יטול ויוציא מתחת ידו.

12. Salary for a son-in-law

☞ *Is Mordy allowed to withhold the money he committed to pay his son-in-law for learning with Yossi?*

Yes, provided two conditions are met: -

1- Mordy had no intention of paying at the original time of the hiring. Rather he merely wanted to encourage his son-in-law to fulfill his Biblical obligation of learning with his son[3].

2- Josh is a man of means. If Josh was a poor person then Mordy's words could be considered as an irrevocable pledge to charity.

Since Josh has a specific *Mitzvah* to learn with his son, his father-in-law or indeed anyone at all is allowed or even required to encourage him to perform that *Mitzvah.* A person who insists he will only do a specific *Mitzvah* if remuneration will be forthcoming can be falsely assured of that money simply to encourage him to act. Being required to act anyway we do not view the worker as working for the money but rather as simply carrying out the pre-existing will of his Maker.

---

3 As is mentioned in the first paragraph of the Shema ושננתם לבניך- and you should learn diligently with your children

איתא ברמ"א סי' פא סעי' א וז"ל מי שאמר לחתנו העשיר תלמוד עם בנך ואני משלם לך פטור כיון דלאו עני הוא ובלא"ה חייב ללמד עם בנו יכול לומר משטה הייתי בך עכ"ל ועי' בש"ך ס"ק ה וז"ל העשיר כו' לאו דוקא אלא ר"ל כל שאינו עני וכו' עכ"ל והקצוה"ח ס"ק ג מבאר הענין יותר וז"ל ודברים אלו לשיעורין דאכתי מנא ידע כמות ואיכות העשיר אבל בתשובת מיימון לס' משפטים סי' סד שם מבואר הענין וז"ל ראובן שנדר לשמעון חתנו ב' ליטרות כדי שיהי' לומד עם בנו ועתה רוצה ראובן לחזור בו כיון שלא הי' קנין בדבר וכו' אם שמעון ירד כ"כ מנכסיו עד שלא היה לו מאתים זוז כו' אז כל מה שנדר לו חמיו בדיבור בעלמא חייב ליתן וכו' דמחוייב לקיים מטעם נדר עכ"ל.

וע"ע שם ס"ק ד שכתב שיכול לומר משטה הייתי בך וכו' ומסתמא כיון להשטות וכו' אך אם הוא בעצמו שיודע כוונתו שלא כיון להשטות צריך הוא לשלם לפי שנתחייב בשכירות וכעין זה איתא במחנה אפרים הלכות שכירות סי' טו.

13. Cheesecake

☞ *Leah insists that her husband is the rightful benefactor of Pierre's generosity both with the platter and the price discount. Is she correct?*

She is at least half wrong.

Tzvi is not allowed to charge Levi more than forty dollars for each cake[4]. Acting only as an emissary he is not authorized to profit on the deal and can charge no more than he was charged.

The platter presents more of a Halachic difficulty. Not being part of the original deal, Tzvi may be entitled to a share in it, or even to keep it entirely. The crucial factor to identify here is the intention of the seller.

While it is clear the gift was given as a gesture of Pierre's amorous affection for Tzvi, this may still only suffice to entitle Tzvi to a half share in the platter. Being received as a direct product of the business transaction, Mona, who instigated that transaction would also be entitled to a share in the platter. Only if the gift is totally divorced from the sale would the emissary be entitled to keep it in full.

---

4 See also Destination Beijing p. 232

איתא בכתובות צח׳ א׳ תניא הוסיפו לו אחת יתירה הכל לשליח דברי רבי יהודה רבי יוסי אומר חולקין והתניא רבי יוסי אומר הכל לבעל המעות אמר רמי בר חמא לא קשיא כאן בדבר שיש לו קצבה כאן בדבר שאין לו קצבה.

והרי״ף שם כ׳ וז״ל והוסיף לו אחת יתירה חולקין ולמה חולקין השליח עם בעל המעות הואיל ובאתה לו לשליח הנאה על ידי בעל הבית חולק עמו עכ״ל וכ׳ הר״ן שם מלשון הרי״ף נראה שדבר שיש לו קצבה אפי׳ נתן המוכר לשליח בפירוש כיון שבאת הנאה לשליח ע״י בעל הבית חולק עמו עכ״ל.

ורש״י שם ד״ה שיש לו קצבה כתב טעם אחר וז״ל דמתנה הואי יש לומר לשליח נתנה ויש לומר לבעל מעות נתנה עכ״ל.

ועי׳ בשו״ע סי׳ קפג סעי׳ ו שהמחבר סותם כדעת הרי״ף אבל הרמ״א כתב מיהו אם אמר המוכר בפי׳ שנותן לשליח הכל של שליח עכ״ל והסמ״ע ס״ק יח כתב דאף שמור״ם סתם כדעת רש״י מ״מ לפעמים לפי ראות הדיין יש לסמוך על טעם הרי״ף (והרא״ש והעיטור) וכ׳ עליו הט״ז שיפה כתב דדעת רש״י נחשב כדעת יחיד נגד כמה ראשונים שסוברים כהרי״ף.

ומ״מ הסמ״ע שם ס״ק כב הביא מתשובת הרשב״א המיוחסות לרמב״ן סי׳ ס שאלה אם הקהל מינו את ראובן בגביית המס ולפרוע להשר מה שיגבה והשר קיבל הפירעון וההנהו משלו במעות והקהל אומר לראובן מה שנתן לך השר קנינו אותה מתנה וראובן טוען המתנה לא באה לידי בסבתכם אלא לפי שההניתי אותו ושהייתי מלוה לו משלי כשלא היה בידי ממון מגביית המס הדין עם מי.

תשובה מסתברא הדין עם ראובן ואף על פי ששנו....דבר שיש לו קצבה חולקין דבר שאין קצבה הכל לבעל המעות כבר פירש הגאון רב האי ז״ל בספר מקח וממכר בשער ו׳ טעם דבר שיש לו קצבה לפי שכל חפץ שדמיו קצובין כשמוסיף עליו הלוקח מרצון נפשו הוסיף וכאילו נתנו בפני עצמו לשליח, או יש לומר שלא הוסיף אלא מחמת שלקח ממנו זה החפץ ונמצא של בעל המעות הוא ומשום הכי חולקין עכ״ל ומכאן שכל דבר שנותן ללוקח שלא מחמת מקח וממכר ושאין בו הטעם הזה שכתב הגאון הכל לשליח ורש״י ז״ל פירש שיש לו קצבה משום דמתנה הויא ויש לומר לשליח נתנה או לבעל הבית נתנה ולפיכך חולקין. ולפי פירוש זה בנדון שלפנינו מי שנותן בפירוש לשליח הכל לשליח. והרב בעל העיטור כתב הטעם לפי שבאה לשליח הנאה על ידי בעל הבית לפיכך חולק עמו.....ואפילו כן בכאן הכל לשליח כיון שהוא טוען שהוא ההנה את השר להלוות לו ושהוא נתן לו בפירוש ולא לציבור עכ״ל .

ולפ"ז בנידן דידן צריך להבין היטב הטעם אמאי נתן המוכר הצלוחית לשליח בחנם דבהשקפה ראשונה נראה דדומה ממש לתשובת הרשב"א דכל כוונת המוכר רק ליהנות ידידו השליח ולא נתן הצלוחית מחמת קניית העוגה, ומוכרח שכן הוא דהלא מכר כמה עוגות כאלו לפני זה ולא נתן צלוחית לקונה אחר בחנם ופשוט שדוקא לו נתן המתנה ורק הוי בסבת שבא לפניו בשליחותו. ז"ש שכל השליחות אינה אלא הוי גורם להנאה וכמו שפשוט שאם מצא השליח מציאה בדרך שליחותו שיכול לזכות בו לעצמו ואין צריך ליתן חלק להמשלח והוא מטעם דמציאת חפץ ברחוב אין לו שום שייכות להשליחות ואינו שייך כלל לציווי המשלח כדי שיוכל לזכות בחלקו ממנו וה"ה כאן.

אבל יש לחקור בדבר דאע"ג דכל כוונת המוכר היא להנות ידידו השליח מ"מ לא נתן לו עצם הצלוחית אלא להיות בסיס להעוגה שקנה בשביל המשלח וא"כ לכאורה י"ל דקבלת הצלוחית בחפצו נובע ממש אך ורק מחמת השליחות אע"פ שמצד ממונות הצלוחית כולה אינו נובע אלא מחמת השליח. אשר על כן כתבתי בפנים דחולקין הצלוחית ביניהם חדא כפי הרי"ף הנ"ל ועוד דאפילו לרש"י יש לצדד דבנדון זה מודה כאן שיש גם להמשלח חלק בו.

וכל ספק זה רק בענין הצלוחית אבל לגבי הממון פשוט שהריוח לבעל המעות דהנה כ' הש"ך סי' קפג ס"ק יז וז"ל ראובן ששלח עם משכנות שלו להלוות לו עליהם מעכו"ם כפי שיוכל להמציא מהם והשליח אומר שהמציא בסך כך וכך וראובן נודע לו אח"כ שלוה בפחות מסך שאמר אין לראובן ליתן כ"א מה שנותן השליח לעכו"ם וכו' והוא פשוט בעיני ונכון עכ"ל.

וע"ע בבאר הגולה אות צ שנתן טעם לדבר וז"ל והיינו משום דהמעות של המשלח והנשאר ברשות דמרא קיימא עכ"ל.

ובזה יש לחלק בין שליח שהרויח דהיינו שקיבל יותר ממה שחשב המשלח ובין שליח ששילם פחות ממה שאמר לו המשלח דבזה אין לו חלק בריוח דאין היתר אלא מעות שלא הוציא מרשות המשלח. וכעין זה מצינו לקמן סי' שלב סעי' ב' אמר לו בעל הבית שכור לי בארבעה והלך השליח ושכר בשלשה אע"פ שמלאכתן שוה ד' אין להם אלא ג' ע"כ ועי' בש"ך שם ס"ק י' וז"ל ונראה שהבע"ה אין צריך ליתן הדינר הד' אף להשליח עכ"ל.

14. Suit Sale Saga

☞ *Whose solution- Fischel's, Ari's or Mendy's, is the Halachically correct one?*

None of them.

Of the three hundred dollar total, Ari should pay one hundred and eighty dollars and Fischel one hundred and twenty.

All the suggested solutions could apply if Ari and Fischel would be considered Halachic partners. Then it would be necessary to calculate how to split the profit gained from the free second suit.

However, not having followed correct Halachic procedure to establish their partnership the two remained separate entities that just *happened* to have bought two suits simultaneously. Therefore they pay proportionately according to the value of their own purchased suits. Since Fischel's suit was worth two thirds of the price of Ari's he pays two thirds of what Ari has to pay.

It is incorrect to argue that Ari has the upper hand because he bought one suit and then got the second one free. Mendy, the storeowner knew that the smaller suit was for Fischel and would never have intended to give Ari possession of it, despite the fact that Ari's credit card was used to make the purchase.

איתא במחבר סי קעו סעי׳ א וז״ל השותפים שבאו להשתתף אין השיתוף נגמר בדיבור לומר שאם אמר בואו ונשתתף יחד בכך וכך שלא יוכלו לחזור בהם ואינו מתקיים אלא בקנין וכיון שצריך קנין כל דבר ודבר לפי קניינו מתקיים שיתופו עכ״ל.

וע״ע במחבר סעי׳ ה השותפין שהטילו לכיס זה מנה וזה מאתים וזה ש׳ ונתעסקו כולם בממון סתם ופיחתו או הותירו השכר או הפחת ביניהם בשוה לפי מנינם לא לפי המעות אפי׳ לקחו שור לטביחה שאלו לא מכרוהו היה נוטל כל אחד מבשרו לפי מעותיו אם מכרוהו חי ופחתו או הותירו השכר או הפחת לאמצע. קנאו שור לטביחה ועומד לטביחה חולקין הריוח לפי מעותיהן אע״פ שבסתם שותפות השבח לאמצע מ״מ ק׳ לומר דהיה לו להתנות שלא יהיו רווחים לאמצע דאין השותפות נעשה אלא אדעתא ליפרד מיד וכן מצינו בנתיה״מ ס״ק ח בתחלת תירוצו וז״ל ....דהא לקחו אדעתא דלחלקו תיכף לאיבריו ומה היה להם להתנות כיון שלא לקחוהו אדעתא דלמכרו ולהרויח בו רק לחלקו ביניהם לאיבריו עכ״ל.

15. A Deathbed Gambit

☞ *Can Daniel and Ezra salvage any more than two million dollars each from their late father's fifty million dollar estate?*

Daniel can and Ezra possibly also.

Although it appeared that Moshe had covered every possibility to ensure the new will could not be challenged there was one fatal flaw in his scheme; he had not given consideration to the fact that Daniel was his father's firstborn.

According to strict Torah law Daniel, being the *bchor,* would receive double the inheritance of his brothers. A standard will, the type that Moshe had Rachamim sign, is insufficient to overrule this Biblical mandate and only the implementation of a special formula would have been able to achieve Halachic complicity. Therefore Daniel's fifty per cent stake in his father's estate remains intact.

Given that the will has now been partly negated vis-à-vis Daniel's portion one now has to consider whether this in turn negates the entire new will, or whether contingency measures will be applied to accommodate the Biblical veto. This question is a matter of dispute between the authorities.

(The technicalities of exactly which assets are included in the Torah mandate of granting a bchor double and which are excluded is beyond the scope of this present work- see Shulchan Aruch ch. 278.)

☙ ☙ ☙

איתא במחבר סי׳ רפא סע׳ ו שכיב מרע שיש לו בכור ופשוטים וריבה לאחד מהפשוטים בלשון ירושה כגון שאמר פלוני בני יירש כך וכך לא אמר כלום וי״א שחלוקת הפשוטים קיימת ומקבצים מכלם לפי חשבון ומשלימים לבכור עכ״ל ועי׳ במגיד משנה פ״ו מהלכות נחלות הלכה ג שביאר וז״ל ....כיון שאמר בלשון ירושה אע״פ שלא הזכיר הבכור בפירוש כיון שמכלל דבריו נגרע זכות הבכור ואמרן בלשון ירושה הרי הוא בכלל לא יוכל לבכר וכו׳ ועוד כתב הרב אבן מגאש ז״ל לומר שכל שיש שם בכור כשם שבטלה צוואתו אצל הבכור כך בטלה אצל הפשוטים ואין בדבריו כלום כיון שאמרן בלשון ירושה. ובזה נחלקו עליו ז״ל קצת מן האחרונים ואמרו שאצל הפשוטים דבריו קיימין עכ״ל. ומבואר דעכ״פ לכו״ע אצל הבכור הצוואה בטלה ולא נחלקו אלא לענין הפשוטים.

וראיתי שאלה זו בספר אורחות המשפטים חלק ג׳ דיני צוואה אות יד בשם מהר״ש חלק ז׳ סימן קנ״ד וז״ל באחד שהיה לו בנים מאשתו הראשונה ובן יחיד מאשתו השניה ופעם עשה צוואה שכל נכסיו יהיו לאשתו אך היא מתה מקודם וירש אותה ואחר כן אמר שמעתה כל בניו ירשוהו בשוה ויען כי היה בביתו רק עם בנו הצעיר לבד ופתאום נחלה על לעהמונג (שיתוק איברים) ובאותו יום עשה צוואה חדשה ונכתב בה שבנו הצעיר יהיה יורש על כל הנכסים, רק מחויב ליתן לאחיו ולאחיותיו סך י״ב אלפים בעד חלקם ונראים הדברים שמחמת ששום אחד מבניו לא היה שם, היה מוכרח למלאות רצון בנו הצעיר וכו׳ ועתה אחר פטירת אביו טוען הבכור שצוואה זו אין בה ממש וכו׳.

הנה באמת צדקו טענת הבכור כי על ידי הצוואה לא יוכל לגרוע כח הבכור, דרק לגרוע כח הפשוט אם לא אמר מקודם לשון לא יירש מהני אבל לגרוע כח הבכור לא מהני רק באמר בפירוש לשון מתנה עכ״ל.

16. Appliance agony

☞ *Is Shimon responsible for the unwanted disposal of the Weissbaum's milchige dishwasher?*

☞ *Would Shimon have been allowed to charge the Weissbaums for the full price of the first dishwasher?*

1- No.

Someone who sells faulty goods is not held responsible for indirect losses associated with that sale (assuming the seller was unaware the goods were faulty.)

Unless Shimon was negligent in supplying faulty merchandise he remains exempt from aggravated expenses.

2- Yes.

However, the Weissbaum's would then have had the option to refuse and simply return the machine. They cannot however demand to keep the machine without additional payment.[5]

ଔ ଔ ଔ

איתא במחבר סי' רלב סעי' כא הלוקח מחבירו והודיעו שהוא מוליכו
למדינה פלונית למכרו שם ואחר שהוליכו לשם נמצא בו מום וכו' ואם לא היה

---

5 see Es-rogue (p.214)

(המוכר) יודע בממכרו שהיה בו מום פטור מהוצאת ההולכה ע"כ וה"ה בנידוננו שלא ידע המוכר שיש מום בהמאשין החדש.

ועוד איתא במחבר סי' רכז בסעי' ז עד מתי יכול לחזור ולתבוע אונאתו וכו' עד כדי שיראה לתגר ובסעי' ח בד"א בלוקח שהרי המקח בידו ומראהו אבל המוכר חוזר באונאה לעולם ע"כ ולכן בנידונינו יכול המוכר לתבוע אונאתו על המאשין הראשון.

17. Exercise and Caution

☞ *Does Nachman have to pay for the theft of the elliptical orbiter and the missing box?*

Partly. He would have to pay for the loss of the orbiter, but not for the box.

It is important here to differentiate between two different types of *shomrim*, guardians. A shomer chinom is someone who guards another's possessions without remuneration, whereas a *shomer sochor* is one who *is* paid for the job.

Since Nachman was looking after the boxes as a favor without pay he is only responsible for losses occurring due to negligence. While although he was not authorized to return the boxes until the Greenstein's return, leaving them in a secure, locked apartment would not be dubbed negligent.

He would, however be responsible for the theft of the elliptical orbiter. Since Nachman was actually using the orbiter, and not merely storing it he assumes the Halachic status of a *sho'el*, a borrower whose responsibilities include loss due to theft.

Had Yehoshua made use of the orbiter contingent upon the storage of the boxes Nachman would have been responsible to pay for the loss of both, the use of the exercise equipment being sufficient remuneration to render him a *shomer sochor* on the boxes.

❧ ❧ ❧

איתא במחבר סי' שמ סעי' א השואל מחבירו בהמה או מטלטלין ונאנסו בידו כגון שמתה או נשבר או נשבה חייב וכו' וא"צ לומר שחייב בגניבה ואבידה ע"כ.

וע"ע בסי' רצא סעי' א שומר חנם פטור בשבועה (עי' סי' רצד) מגניבה ואבידה ואינו חייב לשלם כי אם בפשיעה ע"כ.

ואיתא בסי' שג סעי' ב שומר שכר חייב בגניבה ואבידה ועי' בערוך השלחן סי' שג אות ג אפילו לא שכרו במעות אלא בעד טובה שעשה לו כגון שאומר לו אעשה לך דבר פלוני ותהא לי שומר דינו כשומר שכר דזהו כמו ששכרו בעד זה ע"כ.

ועוד איתא במחבר סי' רצג סעי' א בכל מקום שירצה הנפקד להחזיר למפקיד פקדונו צריך לקבלו אפילו נתנו לו בעל כרחו ואם הפקידו אצלו לזמן ידוע אינו יכול להכריחו לקבלו ממנו תוך הזמן ועי' בקצוה"ח שם ס"ק ב וז"ל ואם הפקידו אצלו לזמן. כ"כ הרב המגיד פ"ז משאלה שיכול לומר קבלת עליך שמירתו עד זמן ידוע.

ובמשנה למלך שם הקשה מפועל דיכול לחזור בחצי היום ע"ש וכבר הקשה קושיא זו ריטב"א פ"ק דקידושין הביא בשם הראב"ד דתוך זמנו אין השומר יכול לחזור והקשה עליו מפועל ע"ש. וכבר כתבנו בישובו בסי' ע"ד סק"א דשומר שאני דנשתעבד נכסי לשלם אם יגנוב או יאבד בפשיעה ואפי' החזירו לבעלים תוך זמנו אם ש"ש הוא ונגנב אצל הבעלים הרי הוא נתחייב בגניבה ואבידה וכו' אם החזיר לבעלים בע"כ אפי' ש"ח לא הוי הבעלים וא"כ כל דין אחריות עליו בין ש"ח בין ש"ש אפי' כשהוא ביד הבעלים עד הזמן שנתחייב בדין שומרים עכ"ל.

וע"ע בספר מחנה אפרים הלכות שומרים סימן יח.

Glossary

Alef	*first letter of Hebrew alphabet; one*
Aufruf	*Sabbath celebration for the groom immediately prior to his wedding*
Avos Ubonim	*fathers and sons (....learning together group)*
Bchor	*first born male*
Beis Din/ Beit Din	*rabbinical court of law*
Beis Hamedrash	*study hall*
Bentching Gommel	*prayer offered as thanks for delivery from a potentially dangerous situation*
Bochurim	*bachelors; Unmarried Torah scholars*
Bris	*circumcision*
Brochos	*blessings; first tractate in the Talmud*
Chaburah	*group of Torah scholars following a specific course of study together*
Chassuna	*wedding*
Chavrusah	*study partner*
Chazer	*review*
Chol Hamoed	*Intermediate festival days*
Cholent	*Shabbos stew*
Chosson	*groom*
Chumash	*Bible*
Daf	*folio*
Daf Yomi	*daily folio study session*
Davening	*praying*
Dayan; Dayonim	*Rabbinical judge; judges*

Din	*judgement*
Din Torah	*court case*
Dira	*apartment*
Divrei Torah	*words of Torah*
Dreidle	*chanukah spinning top*
Droshos	*speeches*
Eishes Chayil	*ballad sung on Sabbath eve in praise of the Jewish woman*
Esrog; Esrogim	*citron; citrons*
Fleishige	*meaty*
Gabbai	*sextant; assistant*
Gemach	*free-loan institution*
Halacha	*Jewish law*
Kaddish	*Prayer recited in memory of the deceased*
Kallah	*bride*
Kiddush	*prayer of sanctification followed by celebratory feast*
Kishke	*stuffed derma*
L'at	*slow down*
L'chaim	*a toast with alcoholic drink*
Lsheim Matzos Mitzvah	*for the sake of matzo observance*
Maariv	*evening prayer*
Mechitza	*separation*
Mesiras Nefesh	*self-sacrifice*
Milchige	*milky*
Min Hashomayim	*with Divine Intervention*
Mishna	*subsection of Talmudic tractate*

Motzei Shabbos	*Saturday night*
Paskened	*ruled*
Pidyon Haben	*first born redemption ceremony performed thirty days after birth*
Pshoro	*compromise solution*
Rosh Chodesh	*New Moon*
Shabbos	*Sabbath*
Shadchan	*matchmaker*
Shidduch	*match*
Shiur	*Torah lecture*
Shlep	*carry, drag*
Shmatte	*old washcloth*
Sholom Aleichem	*Peace unto you*
Shul	*synagogue*
Simcha	*joyous occassion*
Simchas Torah	*closing day of Tabernacle festival when the Torah is completed*
Tess	*ninth letter in hebrew alphabet; nine*
Tosfos	*medieval Talmudic commentary compendium*
Ukatz	*stem*
Yichus	*antecedency*
Yom Tov	*festival*
Zeide	*grandfather*
Zman	*semester*

לע"נ

ר' שמעון בן ר' משה הכהן ז"ל Neumann

ולע"נ

ר' דב אריה בן ר' משה צבי ז"ל Silver

לע"נ

ר' אברהם יצחק בן ר' אריה ז"ל

ר' משה פרץ בן ר' בנימין זאב ז"ל

לע"נ ר' יצחק זעליג ז"ל
בן ר' ישראל שלמה הכהן נ"י

לע"נ מרת שרה בת אפרים ע"ה
ר' יצחק ב"ן משה ע"ה

לע"נ האשה החשובה
חיה שרה בת ר' פסח חיים ע"ה

לע"נ

ר' יהושע בן ר' פרץ ז"ל Tager

נפטר ט"ו אדר ב' תשס"ה

לע"נ

מרת פערל פנינה בת ר' חיים מנחם ע"ה

נפטרה ז' אדר תשס"ו

לע"נ

גמילה בת סולתנא

חנה בת מרים

ר' יוסף הכהן בן חי'